Nothing to Hide

Lesley McGrath Woodley
with Margaret Douglass

Nothing to Hide

A fruitful life

broad continent

Melbourne

First published in 2021
Copyright © Lesley McGrath Woodley 2021
The moral right of the author has been asserted.
All rights reserved. No part of this book may be reproduced or transmitted in any form or by any means, electronic or mechanical, including photocopying, recording or by any information storage and retrieval system, without prior written permission from the publisher.

Broad Continent Publishing
PO Box 198, Forest Hill Victoria 3131, Australia
management@broadcontinent.com.au
www.broadcontinent.com.au

Unless otherwise noted, Scripture quotations are from the Revised Standard Version of the Bible, copyright © 1946, 1952, and 1971 the Division of Christian Education of the National Council of the Churches of Christ in the United States of America. Used by permission. All rights reserved.

Quotations marked NIV are from The Holy Bible, New International Version,® NIV® Copyright © 1973, 1978, 1984, 2011 by Biblica, Inc.™ Used by permission. All rights reserved worldwide.

Quotations marked CEV are from the Contemporary English Version. Copyright © 1991, 1992, 1995 by American Bible Society. Used by permission.

ISBN: 978-0-6484234-1-6 (paperback)

A catalogue record for this work is available from the National Library of Australia.

Cover photograph by Sam Roberts
sam@samroberts.photo
www.samroberts.photo
Telephone +61 415 179 717

Edited by Owen Salter

Foreword

In 2006 Lesley McGrath Woodley was invited to speak at a Unión Bíblica (Scripture Union) conference in Lima, Peru. She returned to Australia in humble astonishment at what she discovered.

In the 1970s, she was the inaugural schools and camps worker for Unión Bíblica in Peru. When she left Peru in 1981 about two hundred children were involved in school and camp activities. She returned to Australia with a sense of abject failure.

On her 2006 visit she discovered that the young people she had mentored had continued the work in accordance with her training, and that under God it had exploded. Thirty-two thousand students were now involved with Unión Bíblica every week, spread out across twenty of Peru's twenty-four provinces and into neighbouring countries.

This book of her recollections and reflections reassures us that when we are committed to serving God wholeheartedly, he works in extraordinary ways, in spite of our weaknesses and failings.

Margaret Douglass

Margaret Douglass is an Arts graduate from the University of Sydney where she majored in English and History. The wife of an Anglican minister and mother of four, she also taught at SCEGGS Moss Vale, Abbotsleigh Wahroonga, and was founding principal of St Luke's Secondary School, Dee Why. She is author of several biographies.

Contents

	Foreword	5
	Prologue	9
1	A replacement?	11
2	A glimpse of South America	19
3	Towards high school	21
4	My understanding expands	23
5	Towards teachers' college	27
6	Secondary teaching	31
7	North Queensland	35
8	Peru beckons, via Moore College	41
9	St Andrew's Hall	49
10	Perfect timing	55
11	The scent of Peru	61
12	Language and culture	69
13	A new home	75
14	Working with Unión Bíblica	79
15	Creativity and pressure	87
16	Camps in quantity	91
17	First home leave	95
18	In Australia	99
19	Return to Peru	103
20	Major expansions	107
21	Bombshell	115
22	Wilderness of misery	117

23	Towards healing	121
24	Refocussing	125
25	More perplexity	129
26	Moving south	133
27	El Salvador and Peru	139
28	Bombshell two	147
29	Wider horizons	151
30	Moving west	153
31	New vistas	159
32	... and new challenges!	163
33	Life changes again	167
34	Purposeful travel	171
35	Ministry to the interior	175
36	Family responsibilities	179
37	Scripture Union South Australia	183
38	Trinity Adelaide and Terrace Studies	185
39	Peru again–with Len	187
40	Mentoring women	191
41	Family drama	195
42	CMS again	201
43	Peru again	205
44	Family farewells	209
45	CWCI	215
46	Farewell to Peru	217
47	2016 Jubilee year	221
48	Encouragement from Peru	225
49	A big move, a big birthday ... and a big surprise	233
	Acknowledgements	237

Prologue

LIMA, 19 NOVEMBER 1980

I received a phone call asking me to come to a meeting with three members of the Unión Bíblica Peru board. I went immediately. I had no idea what it could be about. They gave me the most devastating news of my life to that point. They told me I was to go back to Australia and get help because I showed signs of emotional problems that needed solving.

I knew they were right. All my struggles to get on happily with others showed this. I asked for time to finish the leadership training course I was running. They refused my request and told me I was to leave in a week.

How could this happen? I went home utterly dejected. I felt certain Peru was where God wanted me to be. How could I face my family and friends as such a failure?

My God—where are you?

At eighteen months with Mummy.
1950

ONE

A replacement?

I entered the world at the civilised hour of 9.50 am on Sunday 18 July 1948. I was showered with gifts: a bracelet, bangle and brooch, a drinking cup and a christening robe. I was very much a wanted child.

Because the family occasionally went to the Anglican Church in Toowoomba, I was baptised there on 3 October 1948. The baptism was a family affair: my mother's brother, Uncle Clarence, and his soon-to-be wife became my godparents and, with my parents, made the promises to bring me up as a Christian. Even though they didn't go to church regularly themselves, they made sure, as the years went on, that I attended Sunday school.

My parents, Jim and Jean, were living in my grandmother's house at this time. My grandfather had died just before Dad's return to Australia in 1945 after service in the air force, so Dad had helped his widowed mother buy the home using his service savings. He had been a Wireless Air Gunner (WAG) from May 1942 to September 1945, seeing action in North Africa, the Middle East, Italy and Europe, and visiting many different parts of the world.

My mother didn't find it easy living with her mother-in-law, and it became even more difficult with a newborn baby. So when Dad had the opportunity to transfer to Ipswich as a train guard, he gladly accepted the job. I was six months of age when my parents moved to Silkstone near Ipswich, which was to be my home for the next sixteen years. The two-bedroom house they found was a basic little home of the times, with an entry from the front verandah into the living and dining rooms and through to the kitchen. The kitchen had a door out to the backyard on one side and a hall leading to the bathroom, with bedrooms and an open-sided verandah, on the other side. I had a bedroom all to myself (though that was to change). The laundry and toilet were in the backyard, the latter a fair way from the house for reasons of hygiene. The "dunny can" was collected weekly by men from the local council. I was three when the sewerage was installed, and I liked to play in the sand the workmen were using to lay the pipes.

Being a competent handyman, Dad transformed the house over the years, making it a home for me and my six siblings. He first built a garage, then made the kitchen more functional by giving it new bench space with cupboards underneath. He lined the hall on one side with cupboards reaching to the ceiling for storage, and closed in the side verandah so it became a bedroom for two children. He built beds with shelves in the bedheads for the lucky occupants.

I have been told we had a pussycat named Sandy whom I loved and copied by carrying my toys in my mouth when I crawled. There was great excitement when I pulled myself up to try to walk at eight months, and I finally succeeded during an aunt's visit at eleven months. My first word was "pretty" followed by "mummy", "ta", "birdie" and "pussy". Once I could walk, I spent a lot of time in the backyard watching Dad build the garage. He used to sit me in the wheelbarrow to keep me out of mischief. I loved being wheeled around, and I in turn would wheel a long-suffering Sandy around in the doll's pram Dad had made for me. One day I decided to help him, so I started to climb the ladder to join him. He must have had a fright when he saw me, and he shouted for my mother to come and lift me off as he guided me down.

My first two years seemed idyllic. I was lavished with love by both parents and felt secure and cherished. Four days after my second birthday, my sister, Karen Joan, was born, and I slowly discovered the delights and frustrations of having a younger sibling. The other big news of my third year was a feature article about me in the local newspaper, which read:

> Lesley McGrath, of 33 Cole Street, Silkstone, placed an uncooked green pea in her nostril yesterday while her mother was preparing dinner. The ambulance was called and the child was taken to the Ipswich General Hospital, where the pea was removed.

Karen and Lesley at Lone Pine. 1953

With the family at Rainbow Beach.
1953

For my third birthday, Mummy made me a Bunny ice cream cake. She was proud of me because I knew my alphabet, could count up to ten and rode my bike well.

Once Karen was old enough, she and I used to play outside, dressing up in old clothes, making boats and other things out of boxes and swinging on the swing. Sometimes we played boys' games with the twins from across the road. This was the year I became "Mummy's helper". I was taught to wipe up, dust and run messages for her.

Occasionally, once Karen was old enough and if Dad was scheduled to go to Grandchester, he enjoyed taking Karen and me to work. We would ride with him in the guard's van. Sometimes he would take us up to the locomotive to watch the fireman shovelling coal into the furnace. I loved to pull the cord and hear the whistle pealing across the countryside. We always arrived home covered in soot, and Mummy always complained. We didn't care; we just loved our days out.

Just before my fourth birthday, my second sister, Toni Jacqueline, was born. Mummy still made me a Humpty Dumpty birthday cake, and in baby Toni's pram I found a Hornby trainset as my present. I suspect the gift was chosen because Dad would enjoy playing with it. I still have it.

It was during this year that Karen became a bad asthmatic. For this reason, when Toni was old enough, she moved into my bedroom and Karen was given the newly built room. Karen's frequent illnesses resulted in her being small for her age, so Mummy dressed her in the same clothes as Toni and they looked like twins. I felt the odd one out. I began to worry that I was not quite good enough for my parents, especially my mother. Why had they brought home two other baby girls? I had realised somehow that I was born after my parents had lost twins at birth, and without understanding at all, I started to feel I was their attempt to replace these children. I also felt I must have failed because they now had two more replacements. I decided I had to prove to them that I was good enough.

A couple of times a year we used to catch the train to Toowoomba to visit Grandma McGrath. For my first six years, she would come to us for Christmas and then join us on holidays at Rainbow Bay. Grandma would babysit so my parents could have a holiday. I never understood why Mummy criticised the spicy cupcakes she used to bring for us. A few times I went to stay with Grandma. Her house was built on stilts, and I loved to play in the backyard with its thick grass. The dirt at her house was red, not like our black dirt at home. I didn't have responsibilities in the way I did at home.

I started at Silkstone State School when I was five. There were four Grade 1 classes and forty-five to fifty children in each class. Discipline was strict. Each morning the infants' school gathered on the playground, stood at attention to salute the flag and sing "God Save the Queen", and then, after notices, marched in step to class. We were given little bottles of milk at "little lunch" (sadly often warmed by the sun), and I always had peanut butter or Vegemite sandwiches for lunch.

I had my tonsils removed late that year and spent two days in hospital. I had a very sore throat and was allowed to eat as much ice cream as I wanted. My birthday cake that year was, again, Humpty Dumpty. Each day I spent about half an hour walking to school, and when Karen joined me the following year, we walked together. Whatever the popular game was at the time we played on our way. When yo-yos were "in", Daddy made ours, though I wished I could have a bought one like everyone else's. Karen found school work easier than I did and did not have to work hard to achieve good results.

When Toni turned four, she was sent to kindergarten. Karen and I were so envious that we had missed out on this experience, and each night we asked Toni to tell us in detail everything that happened.

Alison June, my third baby sister, joined the family that year. At Christmas time, Karen, Toni and I were excited to find it was not a chicken-house that Dad had been building in the backyard but a full-sized doll's house. It was fully furnished, with curtains and cushions Mummy made. We loved it. When Alison was big enough, she joined us for many meals eaten in or near our little house.

When I was eight years old, Mum suffered badly from an ulcerated leg and was confined to bed for a long time. I had to be responsible for preparing the school lunches and making sure the younger children had breakfast. I also prepared tea when Dad had to work. Mum could do the peas and beans in bed and Dad always cut the pumpkin before he left, but I would stand on a chair to do the potatoes and then I would cook the meal. I would set the doll's house table next to Mummy's bed and we would have tea there.

I longed to hear my mother say "Well done", but that was not her way. I was striving to be good enough but didn't understand why. I always felt I failed.

Over the next few years, so much of my time was spent looking after the other children that I almost forgot what the backyard looked like. In addition to school, Karen and I became members of the Junior Red Cross and the Girls' Friendly Society (GFS) at the local Anglican church. We also learnt "Art of Speech", reciting poems and performing at eisteddfods. We had limited success, but later in life we agreed that this grounding had served us well.

At Junior Red Cross we were taught how to put on bandages and slings and what to do about cuts and abrasions. I passed my Primary First Aid and Primary Home Nursing Certificates. On Anzac Day on a couple of occasions, I laid one of the wreaths. Mrs Hilda Rasmussen led the GFS, and I enjoyed dressing up in uniform and the weekly variety of games, handicrafts and Bible stories. Three years in a row my parents were financially able to send Karen and me for a week to the annual GFS camp at Halse Lodge, Noosa Heads, which was a great experience.

The doll's house.
1956

TWO

A glimpse of South America

I was only eight when I read a book about a missionary in South America. It was a Sunday school or GFS prize, and I remember promising God that I would serve him there one day. About this time the Methodist church near my school had a children's mission, and I went forward to receive Jesus and a book. I enthusiastically encouraged all my friends at school to go and get a free book!

When I was nine, I was given a bike. This meant I could go riding with my friends, the twin boys from across the road. Sometimes we rode to a certain shop and I would stand guard outside while they went to the back, pilfered empty soft drink bottles and then cashed them in the shop for the deposit. I liked feeling part of their group. Once when I was riding, a car tooted its horn behind me and I fell off, smashing my front tooth and breaking my arm. This was one of the few times I saw how much Mum loved me. The incident also led to my being nick-named "Lesley McGrath, the Toothless Galah".

I was given pocket money but of course it was not enough, so I mowed a neighbour's lawn to get more.

When Mum's sister was being married in Drayton, we were all invited. As a nine-year-old it was exciting to be given a new dress to wear and to find I had a grandfather there I had never heard about. He was married to Grandma Phyllis. This led to my mother and father allowing Toni and me to have several wonderful holidays with Grandpa and Grandma Phyllis on their chicken farm. Sadly, Karen had to miss out on these trips because of her asthma.

My eleventh birthday was the day I went on a bus with our Silkstone Red Cross group to the Fair in Brisbane. I loved ice cream, so when there was an ice cream-eating competition, I eagerly entered. I was undeterred by the fact that I was the only girl. The aim was to eat the ice cream in the fastest time. I lined up on the stage with an ice cream in each hand and ripped off the paper, stuffed them both into my mouth, gobbled and held up my sticks. I had won. My photo was on the front page of the *Sunday Mail* with ice cream all over my face, put there for effect (I had completely swallowed my two).

The amazing prize was an ice cream for every child in the winner's school. Silkstone State School was the largest in Queensland, with over 1700 pupils: the Peters company must have been shocked. Several days later, I was called up at the school parade and applauded, then all were given an ice cream.

We girls were all overjoyed to welcome a baby brother, Ian James. I ran to school to announce this great news. I felt, though, that somehow I was expected to be responsible for him as well as my other siblings.

The Sunday school at All Saints Booval, where I went, had over four hundred children attending, so once a student reached the age of twelve, it was expected that she or he would leave and become part of the church congregation. My parents rarely went to church, but they came to watch me, in my white dress, veil and gloves, be confirmed by the archbishop. Without understanding much, I realised this was a significant event in my life.

The following Sunday, I accepted, without question, that I was to stay home while the others went to Sunday school. My mother chose this time to give me a book to read about menstruation. I was glad she did, because I was very shocked when not long after I had my first period. Apart from showing me where the pads were kept, she was not much help and gave me no idea how long this bleeding would go on for. This only added to my insecurity and feelings of not being good enough. I ended my primary school days feeling that what was expected of me in the family and in life in general was more than I could possibly achieve.

THREE

Towards high school

Every year, I was so glad when the long school holidays were over and I started back at school. I always found school a refuge from the demands of home. In 1960 as a Year 7 student, I felt old enough to try to get a job. I managed to persuade the local newsagent to give me one and I worked for two hours every afternoon and on Saturday mornings. The pay was not much, but it gave me highly valued pocket money. The newsagent allowed me to sample the sweets for sale and I ate more than he realised.

I was selected by my Year 7 class to speak at the annual Oration Competition. Perhaps they remembered that I went to elocution classes. The best speaker in each year would represent the school in the zone competition. I had to speak for three minutes in front of over a thousand students and staff. My teacher tried unsuccessfully to encourage me not to be nervous. I was shaking, and her offered glass of water really didn't help. I did not win and never again entered that competition.

Year 8 was called "scholarship year", and when I completed it, I was able to go to Bremer High School. I was determined to make the most of my time there. I had something we McGrath children were used to: a second-hand uniform. I was glad it included a blazer for winter. This was lovely and warm, and I wore it constantly for four years since it was my only decent coat. I proudly sewed my hockey pocket on when I was awarded it in Year 12. I found it hard to be thankful for people's cast offs. As a fourteen-year-old, I was once made to wear an orange dress with large red flowers and puffy sleeves, which were long out of fashion. My friends made fun of me in a way that just reinforced that I was no good.

Year 9 saw my next big pocket money-making effort. I heard that the local lawn mower shop was organising a promotional race in which competitors had to push a lawn mower for more than three kilometres up a hill. I entered and, as with the ice cream competition, was determined to do well. I ran with all my might and was exhausted but delighted to win the women's section. The money prize was enough to pay for two church camps, so I saved it for that.

The best thing about high school was the sporting program. Hockey was my winter sport, and I practised all week to be ready for the Saturday afternoon inter-school matches in Ipswich. I did this in summer, too, getting ready for vigoro matches: batting was my strength, and I also kept wicket. The only event I was ever the best at was the discus throw. In spite of my failure in Year 7 as a speaker, I joined the debating group and every year was a member of our school team in the Ipswich inter-school debating competitions. I was usually the first speaker. I enjoyed being part of the drama group too. Being tall, I was often given male roles. In Year 11 we presented the one-act comedy *The Dear Departed* for the school Open Day.

Academically, I did quite well and was near the top of my year. As usual, while waiting for the Junior Public Examination results, I was anxious that I would fail and have to leave school. I was thrilled when I found I'd passed and could go on to the senior years. In Year 12 I was awarded the Social Studies prize for my History and Geography results.

On the home front, Debra, my fourth sister, was born when I was fifteen. My responsibilities had grown, not lessened, and my bedroom had to stretch to accommodate another sister. My parents recognised our house was too small, and just after my sixteenth birthday we moved to a bigger home.

FOUR

My understanding expands

From the age of twelve onwards, I became more and more involved in the life of All Saints Anglican Church in Booval. I continued to go weekly to GFS and attended a new Sunday morning Bible study group for girls in Year 6 who were confirmed but not old enough to join the youth group. We met in the rectory and were led by our new minister's wife, Mrs Margaret Douglass.

The Brisbane Billy Graham Crusade in 1959 resulted in a number of older young people joining the Youth Fellowship. The fellowship was keen to get more members, so once we from the rectory group were in Year 7, we eagerly joined. Meetings were at the church on Friday nights. As time went on, I saw the strong faith of the youth group leaders. It was more than just believing and going to church; their faith affected everything they did. I wanted a faith like that. Our rector, Mr Don Douglass, used to drive quite a few young people home after meetings, and I was always the last to be dropped off. So one night I asked him about their faith. He told me about Jesus living in them, but I didn't understand.

When I attended a youth camp at Mount Tamborine, Vic Smith, a Brisbane watchmaker, was the Bible teacher. His talks helped me understand more, and as a thirteen-year-old I made a decision to give my whole life to Jesus. I began to read my Bible and pray daily, as we were encouraged to do. I wanted every one of my friends to know Jesus and kept asking them to youth group.

That year I was also given a Sunday school class of my own in the "big" Sunday school after having led a pre-school class in the infants' Sunday school for almost two years. This extra responsibility helped me decide to go on a Saturday morning to the youth group prayer meeting. I felt I needed the prayer support. The older members belonged to the Church Missionary Society's League of Youth, so I went with them to my first CMS camp that year at Mount Tamborine. CMS became very much part of my future. My group leader at this camp was Faye Cutmore, who encouraged me in my mission interest.

It was when I was in Year 11 that we moved to Booval Street, to a bigger house. It was near the church and next door to the home of the curate, the Rev Jim Stonier, who helped with the youth and children's work in the parish. The parish extended from Booval to Goodna, with six churches for the rector to care for.

Our new home was an old Queenslander type with the laundry underneath. Dad immediately got to work and dug out mountains of earth, then by cementing the inside and entrances built a double garage. It became an acquired skill to drive into this garage. He made changes upstairs too, turning verandahs into bedrooms and even making a sewing room for Mum. For me he built a louvered area under the house with a curtain separating it from the laundry. This gave me a haven for study for the time I lived in Booval.

In January each year, CMS Queensland organised a week-long Summer School where there were daily Bible studies and missionaries from different parts of the world speaking about their work each night. This was attended by families from all over the state. By 1963 my parents had become regular members of Booval church, so when Mr Douglass encouraged Booval families to join him and his family at the 1963 Summer School at Port Macquarie, my parents decided our whole family should go. The eight of us crammed into our small Vauxhall Victor, our camping gear packed onto a roof rack. We travelled at night in heavy rain and were very relieved to arrive safely at the camping grounds. Mum was decidedly frustrated with trying to set up camp in the rain. Everything was wet, but someone kindly took us into dry quarters until the rain stopped, when we returned to a dry tent and really enjoyed our week.

John Stott from England led the studies on John chapters 13 to 17, and I loved listening to the missionary talks. I had never forgotten the book I read as an eight-year-old and was again feeling I would one day be an overseas missionary. I prayed, "As I look to the future, Father, I give myself to you for your use. I want to continue to grow in faith and learn to pray with thanksgiving."

I was in Year 11 when Grandma McGrath died. She was seventy-four. Dad held me close and we cried together. I was the only grandchild to go to Toowoomba for her funeral. This was my first experience of a burial, and I sobbed out loud when I heard the thud of the dirt dropped onto the coffin. Later in that year, Andrew John, my sixth sibling, was born. An old life finished and a new one began.

After my seventeenth birthday, Dad took me for a few driving lessons, and quite quickly I passed the driving test and had my licence. Soon after he bought a new family car and gave me the Vauxhall Victor. I was the only girl in Year 12 driving to school, and I used to take my friends out at lunchtime. It was fun.

I spent a lot of time in my senior years trying to work out what to do with my life. I decided to train as a teacher so that I could go to Peru as a missionary. I studied hard and expected to do well enough to win a scholarship to teachers' college. I did not. I made up my mind to repeat Year 12 but then found out I could sit for a supplementary exam in Maths. This I did, and passed. I then had only one more subject to do to get into teachers' college.

I questioned why God had allowed this failure when I was so sure I should go to teachers' college. Mr Stonier told me to trust that God knew what he was doing. He suggested I get a job and study at night school. I went home and thought about that.

In Bremer High School uniform.
1962

FIVE

Towards teachers' college

I decided to follow Mr Stonier's advice and applied for a position in the circulation department at Queensland University library. This job enabled me to study French and Ancient History at night school. My aim was to improve my matriculation score and try again to win a scholarship to Kelvin Grove Teachers' College. The time in the library taught me a lot about books and something about university social life. I was invited to a wine and cheese party, but I didn't drink alcohol and was taken aback by the amount my quiet library colleagues drank and how raucous they became as the evening went on.

Paul, a friend from Bremer High, was in one of the university colleges. He invited me to his room to listen to classical music. He had decorated the room with red cellophane. We had an enjoyable evening but he didn't invite me again, and I was thankful. Perhaps he picked up that I was focused on the mission field, or perhaps I didn't understand what he really intended.

This was the year I first directed a GFS camp at Mount Tamborine. On the way there, I foolishly decided to tell the forty girls on the bus to leave their luggage and hike around the headland to the campsite. At one point a number of them stumbled on a massive ant nest and were badly bitten. Then we had to find a rope to help quite a few climb a steep incline. I had much to learn about leading camps, and at the time thanked God that he had protected us and no one was badly hurt.

Since I had now sold the car I used at school, travelling home after night school at 10 pm involved a bus to the station, a train to Booval and a walk home. My parents were anxious about my safety on the train, so Dad bought a 1956 Austin A40 and informed me I had a loan of $300 to pay off. This was a challenge as I only earned $39 a week and had other expenses. The car got well used travelling back and forth from Booval to Brisbane. One night I ran out of petrol on the way home—someone had milked my tank. I had a long walk to find a telephone, and every time I saw a car coming, I hid in fear. I was so thankful when Dad came and rescued me.

Still not trusting my ability, I was amazed and delighted at the end of the year when I found I had passed my two subjects and been given a scholarship to start at Kelvin Grove in the two-year course to become a primary school teacher. My university library friends gave me a book, *Search the Scriptures,* as a farewell gift since I would no longer be working with them during the day. I still needed to earn money, though, so I was given a job in the library at night and on Saturday mornings. This worked out well as the library was not overly busy at these times and I was able to study while earning needed finance.

As soon as I arrived at teachers' college, I joined the Christian fellowship (TCCF) and revelled in the friendships and Bible studies. Camps, which I always so much enjoyed, were a big part of their program. Once my mother volunteered to be our camp cook. So often I had felt unloved by her, but her offering to cook helped me begin to understand that she showed her love by doing. I was also surprised to realise that I was quite like her.

For the next two years I spent four days each week attending lectures in the variety of subjects primary school teachers must be familiar with. The fifth day was given to "prac teaching" in primary schools, first at Darra and then, in second year, at Graceville. In my first year at Kelvin Grove, my lecturers, to my surprise, suggested I apply for a scholarship to study Physical Education at the University of Queensland. This I hesitantly did. I couldn't see how PE could possibly fit into my missionary plans, but I felt I had to apply, trust God and see what happened.

In my second year at college I met Robyn Lanham, a commerce student, who became a close lifelong friend. Robyn loved me unconditionally, and because she listened, she recognised that, despite my outward show, I often felt desperate inside—even at times to the point of wondering if life was worth living at all.

Robyn and I enjoyed bush walking and camping. One time, along with another friend, Christine Hudson, we hiked to the Stinson plane wreck in Lamington National Park. We made camp on the first night, heating rocks to keep our feet warm. Next day we hacked our way up a steep, wet, heavily overgrown track that we weren't even sure was the right one. It was dark when we reached the top. There to greet us was a blazing fire with a group of men around it. Yes, we had reached the wreck, and thankfully the men were very friendly, giving us one side of their fire as our sleeping quarters. The next day we had fun sliding down the steep, muddy Christmas Creek path. It was a great time of freedom, friendship and enjoying God's creation. We decided to try to return to Lamington Plateau every long weekend, and this we did for some years.

At the beginning of my second year, I heard I had been given the PE scholarship. I attended Physiology and Anatomy lectures on Monday and Wednesday nights and PE theory and practice on Tuesdays and Saturday mornings. On Saturday afternoons I played hockey for the university team. Having Fridays and Sundays free, I was able to continue my GFS work and be actively involved in All Saints' Youth Fellowship. It was a heavy program, and Robyn's friendship helped me through a demanding year.

The news that I had graduated from teachers' college and was one of only two who were given immediate appointments was exciting. I was to work in the Ipswich circuit, teaching swimming in Terms 1 and 3 and visiting primary schools to teach PE during the winter term. The news was not so good from the university's PE department. I had failed Anatomy and had to sit for a supplementary. During college years I had become more involved with Scripture Union and their camping program, but this meant I had to withdraw from the camp I was going to attend as a leader. I was very thrown by this setback and kept asking God what he was trying to teach me. Was I wrong to be doing the PE degree? I sat the exam at the end of January, passed and decided to go into second year and see what happened.

I turned twenty-one in 1969. My students at East Ipswich Primary School did not know this was an important day for me, but my friends did because they were coming to a special birthday party. I prayed, "Thank you, Lord, for all you have taught me up till now. Help me to follow you always and bring others to know you."

The lawnmower race.
1962

SIX
Secondary teaching

In spite of not yet completing my Physical Education course, in 1970 I was appointed as the girls' PE teacher at Ipswich High School. I threw myself into the role, aiming to equip each girl to enjoy PE and discover her potential. One plump girl I taught went on to become a state champion in archery. Ipswich High had not won the Inter-School Athletics Carnival for some time, so I began before-school training for the age relay teams. I taught the skill of securely passing the baton in the circular relay, and we practised over and over again. As the weeks rolled on, the girls grew in fitness, skill and confidence.

On the day of the carnival, Ipswich High won enough minor individual events that the circular relays would decide the winner of the Cup. First the Under 12s lined up. The starter's gun sounded. The first change went well and the second and the third. Ipswich High students were on their feet cheering. The team won. Then the Under 13s won, the Under 14s came second and the 14s came first. Then came the final event of the day, the open relay race. The cheering was deafening. Ipswich High girls ran and passed their batons magnificently, and won. This meant the miracle had happened: they took home the Inter-School Athletics Cup. It was some very proud girls who presented the Cup to the school the next morning at parade. The teamwork and practice had paid off.

I was also keen to teach my students how to pass on the Christian baton by teamwork and practice. I had learnt so much from camps that I decided to hold an athletics camp with leaders recruited from among my Christian friends. I prayed that the girls would see Christ in us and that we would have an opportunity to share Jesus with them. This would be Ipswich High's first-ever school camp. We went to Tallebudgera. Being a state school, we were not allowed to teach the Bible, but I made a point of saying goodnight to every girl when she was in her bunk and speaking a word of encouragement for the progress she had made. The camp was a great success. Later in the year, fifteen students went to Mount Victoria in the Blue Mountains, and four girls wrote to me:

> We're having a great time but it hasn't snowed yet. Yesterday we went to Jenolan Caves. All the leaders are great fun. One week and we will be back to school and our favourite teacher, Miss McGrath. Supper is on but I'm still full from tea …

This opened the way for me to suggest that students go to Scripture Union camps. When I later had my first experience of directing an SU camp, a large number of my students attended. The camp, held on the Brisbane River, was called "Camp Exodus". The brochure made it clear there would be discussions on Christianity as well as canoeing, hiking, swimming, cooking and absolutely no mod cons. Every morning we sang songs and discussed the Bible while at night leaders shared around the campfire how they had come to know Jesus. Despite an episode with a snake, the girls greatly enjoyed the camp, and I felt seeds were sown that would bear fruit.

One day I received a notice announcing an Inter-School Cross Country competition being run in Brisbane. The school principal agreed that I should take a busload of girls to run. The forty-five students I chose were excited. I knew none of them could win, but to my surprise our school did win because so many crossed the finish line and earned points. Most schools sent only two or three runners.

In November 1970 I faced my final university exams. Because I had failed a subject the year before, I told God in my prayers that I felt scared and asked him to help me study well and express what I knew in the exams. Just after Christmas, Robyn and I drove with another friend, Pam, to the CMS Summer School at Katoomba in the Blue Mountains. Yet another friend, Barbara Darling, and her friend Felicity Fries joined us there. John Stott was the Bible teacher again. Unfortunately I became sick and had to fly home while my friends drove my car back to Queensland. They cared for me so lovingly that

I missed them very much, for my mother received me in her usual matter-of-fact way.

News that I had passed all my exams and had graduated with a Diploma of Physical Education was great. I returned to school full of enthusiasm, knowing I could put even more into my work now that I didn't have to go to Brisbane for night lectures. My very full and fairly stressful program was over.

In April the principal called me into his office. It was a shock when he handed me a transfer notice to Pimlico High School in Townsville. I had just over a week to get there and take up my duties. It was only four weeks till the May holidays, but I was not allowed to wait until then to move. I was devastated. I told each of my classes that I was leaving, and I was overwhelmed by the gifts the girls gave me and the notes of appreciation and good wishes I received.

The move meant leaving not just Ipswich High but my parents, six siblings, home and church as well. I could not understand why God was moving me when I felt he was using me so much at Ipswich. But I realised I had no choice. I had to go where I was sent and somehow trust him.

Lesley and Ian at Lone Pine.
1962

SEVEN

North Queensland

Within days I was on *The Sunlander*, heading north by train to Townsville and, for me, into the unknown. I had contacted David Johnson, the Scripture Union Northern Region worker, asking him if he could find me somewhere to board. I was very apprehensive about boarding but had no other choice. He found me somewhere within walking distance of Pimlico High. I planned to return to Booval in the May holidays, collect more of my belongings and drive back with them, trusting by then I would have found a flat to rent, and hopefully a friend to share it with me. The boarding situation proved to be awful—my landlady had strict and, I felt, unreasonable rules. So I was delighted when I learned that Diana Atkinson, a Nurses Christian Fellowship worker who had just come to Townsville, was also looking for someone to share with.

Pimlico High was much bigger than Ipswich High and I was one of five PE staff. There was no way I could do what I had done at Ipswich. My classes were to be for both boys and girls. I had to ask God to give me new ways to serve him.

Diana and I found a flat that was the upstairs part of an old house. In the May holidays I headed south. My mother decided that it would be a good idea for the family to have a holiday in Cairns so that Dad could drive back with me to Townsville, help me settle into my new home and then join them. The two-day, 1000-kilometre drive north with Dad in my car laden with household and personal belongings was special. I so appreciated his willingness to help me set up the flat, the sharing of his thoughts and experiences as we talked, and the very practical driving tips I learnt—especially on the 200-kilometre "horror stretch" between Rockhampton and Mackay where a truck, travelling fast in the opposite direction, forced us off the road.

I soon discovered Pimlico High didn't have a Christian group. I heard of a Christian, Kathy Connolly, in another staffroom, so I visited her and asked her to help me start an Inter-School Christian Fellowship (ISCF) group at the school. Kathy, a quiet Brethren girl, later admitted she was nonplussed when I asked her, but she agreed, and with the help of my Scripture Union friend, David Johnson, a small group started.

Being a nurse, Diana was away from our flat a lot, and at times I felt very lonely. I often drove the winding road to the summit of Townsville's famous Castle Hill and sat on a rock, looking towards the house and waiting for her to return. I desperately missed my family and friends. I asked Kathy if she would like to move into the flat with us and was delighted when she said yes. It was not long before we realised there were other young, lonely, single teachers in Townsville, so we started to invite some to lunch on the weekends or to dinner at night. We asked our guests if they would like to join us as we studied the Bible, and to our joy a number did.

Because I had been so much part of All Saints Booval, I naturally went to the local Anglican church, which was only about two kilometres from our flat. I expressed interest in joining one of their Bible studies and was told they didn't have such groups, so I started a small one. We began by studying Romans. I was shocked when the curate told the people in a sermon that they should not be studying the Bible. Despite this, the group continued to meet, and when I became a CMS missionary years later, they supported me.

To alleviate my loneliness and give myself some relaxed personal sport, I joined a canoe club. I had the opportunity to use their fibreglass moulds to build myself a kayak and paddles. It was thrilling shooting the rapids in my very own canoe. I went on some great trips with the club and later used my canoeing skills at Scripture Union camps.

SU camps had played a big part in my Christian life and in the lives of the girls at Ipswich High. As I spent time with David and his wife, Lorelle, I told them of my experiences. David asked me to help develop camping in his Northern Region. SU used a campsite at Picnic Bay on Magnetic Island, a short ferry ride from Townsville, and I started helping to plan and run the programs there, encouraging students from school to attend. We hiked, swam and had fun, with Bible study

Camp leader.
1969

Teaching discus technique.
1970

and singing as key ingredients.

As a PE teacher, my aim, as in Ipswich, was to help each student reach his or her physical potential and to learn to work in teams. I decided to organise an inter-class volleyball competition in the lunch hour. I worked out a handicap system so that the Grade 8s would not be daunted by the Year 11s. It was a great success, and I was delighted when our Year 10 team joined the town competition.

At the end of the school year, while other teachers were marking exam papers, I asked some Year 10 students who were interested in jazz ballet to help me mobilise students to learn a massive rhythmical movement display to be performed in the school parade ground during the final week. A large number took part. The staff were thankful the students were occupied and the performance was a great success. When school closed for the year, I wrote in my diary:

> So many new things this year. Your timing was absolutely perfect! Thank you for the way you led me. The teachers' Bible study group, the way it started at our place. The way we got to know Ruth; she became involved, then was transferred to Mt Isa. For Marie and the way you worked in her. It's tremendous to be able to get ISCF going here; to see kids getting keen; to see those who've come to know you, going on as Christians. All this is your work. Also there is the Bible study group at St Matthew's. Good to have people who were willing to study Romans. It's been good to be part of planning SU camps up here then co-direct. Thank you, Lord. Are you wanting me somewhere else or am I to stay here? Is it right? I don't want to go to South America, but if it is what you want, Lord, then I am prepared. Lord, help me trust you more and more. Like the song says, "I want to burn out for you."

My holidays were spent enjoying time with my family and friends at All Saints church and at an ISCF camp and the CMS Summer School, which had become annual holiday fixtures. I listened with special interest to the missionaries working in South America and arranged to receive their newsletters. My friend Barbara Darling was teaching at Port Macquarie, and we enjoyed getting together in the holidays and sharing our experiences.

In spite of looking forward to returning to Townsville, I still remembered my plan to be a missionary, and I did not want to be in the wrong place. I wondered if I should be going to Bible college. I talked things over with the Rev Herb Robey, our Booval rector, and he suggested I begin to study through Moore College by post, doing one subject. He offered to be my supervisor. I chose to do New Testament, and Barbara decided to do it too. We were able to encourage one another by mail.

Not long after starting the new year at Pimlico High, another teacher and I took two carloads of students south to an ISCF leadership camp. The ISCF group was becoming a real part of the school, and by March I was sure I was in the right place. As the year went on, my SU camping work grew and the young people who came were blessed. I longed for all the kids around me to come to know Jesus and could not understand why all Christians didn't seem to think evangelism mattered very much. I persuaded some of my friends to join me in running workshops on evangelism. I felt inadequate and ineffective myself—at times I seemed to grow in my love and knowledge of God and at other times I felt I was stagnating. I was aware that I had so much to learn.

EIGHT

Peru beckons, via Moore College

I had a growing interest in South America and regularly heard from missionaries about Peru. I wrote to Hilary Doig, a CMS missionary working with Scripture Union Peru, to ask about the work there. She replied: "The situation is continually changing so it is hard to be specific. Anything could happen to change things—within SU or external things like governments." She told me of the need for SU Peru's camping program to be expanded and encouraged me to pursue theological study to complement my teaching experience. "The more training you get the better," she explained. "Keep open to God's leading. SU work requires infinite patience and flexibility as well as learning to mix with all types of people on the social scale."

I began to consider leaving teaching and going to Deaconess House in Sydney the next year. Students at Deaconess House studied theology at Moore College. I found this a hard possibility to contemplate. I loved teaching. So I prayed, "Jesus, please reveal your will for me in your way. Make me patient to wait for it." I thought: I will probably be back here because I can't see how I can possibly pay for further training.

I contacted CMS and they sent me an "application to serve" form to fill in. I found this a huge, time-consuming task. The questions were very penetrating, and being busy planning end-of-year school activities, organising the camps I was to lead and preparing to speak at the combined end-of-year ISCF breakup, it took me some time to complete. I finally sent it off.

During this second year at Pimlico High, as well as seeing my PE students reaping the benefits of the programs I introduced, I had a number of other new experiences. I was asked to adjudicate the interschool folk dancing at the Charters Towers Eisteddfod. I found this a very difficult job. The disappointment of those who didn't win made me feel bad. I resolved never to accept an invitation to be an adjudicator again. I was also part of a panel on "The Role of the Family in the Community Today" organised by Aitkenvale Methodist Church, and when I was asked to speak at Heatley Mothers' Union, I took a group of young people with me to share what a difference ISCF had made to them. I was very involved in planning a combined ISCF weekend seminar at which Michael Bennett, the ISCF staff worker from Brisbane, was the main speaker. Through this I became involved with Helen and John Lucas in kicking off "Out of School Happening" in the North. I felt fulfilled in my work in Townsville.

When CMS wrote accepting me as a missionary candidate and telling me I was to study for two years at Deaconess House, I knew I was going to resign from the Education Department. I prayed: "How many really understand the agony, trauma in making these decisions? I'm feeling inadequate, yet I know if I keep looking at myself I will be dragged down. My God, I praise you. You are greater than anyone else. You are in control and you allow to happen what is best for us. Please care for all those I am leaving. Keep them, Father."

I applied to Deaconess House, was accepted and headed south. After some years as a teacher I was very nervous about becoming a student again, and also about leaving my home state and living in Sydney.

Mary Andrews was the principal of Deaconess House. She had herself studied there in the 1930s following her training at Gladesville Psychiatric Centre and studies at Sydney Missionary and Bible College. Mary spent time working among the poor, the sick and those who had suffered great injustice. She fought hard against what she called the "powers of darkness" around her. This impulse to work selflessly for the gospel continued when Mary felt the call of God to mission work in China in 1937. Hearing the call to mission work, she courageously went alone to China in 1937, and her amazing stories of God's enabling are still an encouragement to outgoing missionaries today. Because of war, she had to flee in 1944 from China to India, where she worked for some years in a home for destitute women and children. She returned to China in 1947 but again had to leave when the communists came to power. She was appointed Deaconess House principal in 1952.

As a student in 1973, I found many of the rules very old fashioned. We had to be home at night by 10 pm and up by 6.30 am ready for breakfast and chapel. We each had our chores to do in cleaning the house, and Deaconess Andrews made sure they were done perfectly. We attended lectures with the men in nearby Moore College each morning from Tuesday to Friday, but we were only allowed to interact with them at morning tea and once a month in their common room. After the freedom I had enjoyed in Townsville, I found it hard to adapt to these restrictions.

We had lots of assignments to complete, so I spent most afternoons in the library, writing out important information by hand. The cost of the photocopier was prohibitive, and I lived within a strict budget. Not having a typewriter, my essays had to be handwritten.

In my camp work, I had used my guitar to lead singing around the campfire, so when I realised that a number of my Deaconess House colleagues had good singing voices, I started a choir, which I accompanied. We sang at our daily chapel services. Occasionally we joined the Moore College men for supper. One time, when members of the Liturgical Commission were present, one gentleman was asked to lead in "a word of prayer" at the end, and I said, "Make sure it's only a word." Stunned silence was the response, and I realised I had put my foot in it. All the feelings of worthlessness and failure that so often attacked me resurfaced.

All theological students were assigned to a parish for practical experience. We were to help with the youth groups on Friday nights and attend Sunday services. I was sent to St Mark's Darling Point, which was in a wealthy suburb. I found the youth group a challenge. The young people had little understanding of life beyond their affluent suburb and private schools. One wintery Sunday morning, as I stood shivering outside the church, a lady told me I should have a thick coat with a fur collar. I was tempted to ask her to please buy me one!

Everything I was experiencing, especially rubbing shoulders with other Christians, made me again acutely aware of my failings. I wrote in my diary:

> Deliverance, Lord
> That's what I want
> To become, to be made free,
> Free from sin, the shame and the guilt
> Which continually keeps hindering me.
> I come and I claim
> Then turn and reject
> Making your glory my own
> Motives impure impinge and obstruct
> Hindering my walk with you.
> Take my life, Lord
> To you I yield all.
> Make me always to be
> Focused on you, my risen Lord
> In whom there is victory.

One of the great moments of this first year in Sydney was the news that my sister Karen, who by now was married and living in Adelaide, had given birth to a baby girl, Melanie. I was so excited that I ran through the house telling everyone. Karen asked me to be Melanie's godmother, and I went to Adelaide for the baptism held at St Jude's Brighton.

At the end of the year Deaconess Andrews called me into her study. I thought: Now what have I done wrong? I was astounded when she asked me to be the 1974 Senior Student. It was an honour with huge responsibilities. I knew it meant no more sleeping late—I would have to be in her study each morning at 6.30 for prayer. But what a privilege this was! Years later I was asked to speak on prayer, and because I admired Deaconess Andrews so much, I wrote asking her to describe her prayer life so that I could share it. She sent me a postcard: "I seek to make prayer my first work, my most important work, my most persistent work. Love, Mary."

Burdekin River rapids.
1973

In the holidays I headed home to Queensland. My first priority was to find a job so I could survive financially. I was soon working as a nurse's aide in Bardon Maternity Hospital. I loved the work, particularly the joy of witnessing a birth. I realised I could easily have followed my mother and become a nurse. I knew, though, that teaching would always be my first love.

I hadn't been home long when the rest of the family (except Alison) set off to see Karen in Adelaide. Soon after they left the rains came, resulting in the devastating Brisbane flood of January 1974. Churches played a key role in helping those in need. All Saints Booval asked me to coordinate their relief work. This entailed locating places where the homeless could go, getting help with evacuations, finding equipment for the clean-up and organising meals for the relief teams. Added to this, our home became the base for two evacuated families. The clean-up was massive, and because Alison cut her foot after jumping into the edge of the flood waters, she was unable to help. I gave her the job of answering the phone. The family arrived back to find they were sharing their home with the evacuees. Naturally, they immediately joined the clean-up teams. Ian became the deliverer of meals to the workers.

In February, when things had returned to some sort of normality, I went for a short, proper holiday on the Sunshine Coast. I needed that to prepare me for the busy year ahead in Sydney.

I returned to Deaconess House to find that there were fewer theological students than usual and Deaconess Andrews had taken in overseas students as boarders. One of my jobs as senior student was to make sure everyone's chores were done before breakfast. I often found it easier to do a duty myself than to get the boarders out of bed. Another responsibility was to make a roster of "preachers" for the daily chapel service and allocate the topic. I chose Hebrews 11, which challenged people to prepare sermons on different Old Testament characters.

In September I was privileged to be asked to give the address at the Deaconess House Graduation. I did not anticipate the opposition from some men, who were incensed that a woman had been allowed to teach the Bible in front of the archbishop. Archbishop Marcus Loane's response was to invite me to lunch. The Loanes were so gracious and kind that I quickly felt at ease with them.

I had received a number of offers of post-study employment with Scripture Union and various parishes, but I still felt sure I was to be a missionary in South America. CMS had no one serving there and said they were not prepared to send me. Towards the end of the year, I struggled to study and felt unsure about my future. I found, with all the stress, that I had some clashes with friends in the August holidays. I prayed to learn to love, and for the ability to trust for my future. I sensed my relationship with God was out of kilter.

By September 1974 I heard that CMS were again prepared to send missionaries to South America. With exams looming, I found it hard to concentrate. Where would I be next year? Was I ready to go overseas? I just wanted to run away. I knew I was a failure and not good enough, and I got irritated with small things that didn't matter. I needed time to pray, so I decided to take a day off and went to Manly by myself. Walking on the beach calmed me down, and I came back determined to try to pass the exams that were so close. I asked God to show me that I was on the right path and wondered how he would do this.

I applied to CMS Queensland and was interviewed. In her reference, Mary Andrews highlighted my weaknesses, and the whole process brought back the feelings that I was a replacement and not good enough. I was told the committee was unsure and needed time to consider and pray. They would be in touch. I kept telling myself to trust God, but it was an awful time. I walked for hours on Caloundra beach, praying the committee would make the right decision.

At home in Booval.
1976

NINE

St Andrew's Hall

In mid-January 1975 the decision arrived. I was to go to St Andrew's Hall, the CMS training college in Melbourne, and complete my Diploma of Theology (DipTh) at Ridley Theological College. I thanked God. My calling was confirmed.

Even though I was to be in Melbourne by the end of February, Mum and Dad left by car to go to Adelaide again, leaving me to care for my younger brothers and sister. I felt they were reinforcing the message I had heard as a little girl, that I was meant to be "mother" to my siblings. I found I was bored being a "housewife", but somehow I managed. When I finally left for St Andrew's Hall, it was with mixed emotions—sadness mingled with joy, a sense of loss mixed with gain. I prayed, "Teach me, Father, to forget myself and give pre-eminence always to you."

I set out for Melbourne feeling nervous. I had never been to Victoria, and I was unsure how I would relate to those I would be living with. I so often ended up in arguments with people and then felt unworthy and hopeless. I knew some of my Deaconess House fellow students were also CMS candidates and would be at St Andrew's Hall, so some would know me quite well.

St Andrew's Hall was a beautiful Victorian house in Parkville, a delightful Melbourne suburb. CMS offered a pre-departure program for missionaries and, during their time there, students were more fully assessed for their suitability for missionary service.

I was pleased to find that completing my DipTh would not be difficult. Ridley College was next door to St Andrew's Hall. I was thrilled to find that Barbara Darling had also decided to complete her studies there. We were very different people and had had our conflicts at times—we had never lived close to one another and I wondered how being neighbours would work out. I am pleased to say that we found our relationship strengthened, gaining new dimensions of closeness during our time in Melbourne.

All my fellow students seemed to know where they were going and their areas of missionary service. I was confident Peru was my future. Soon after I arrived in Melbourne, however, I was told that, since all their missionaries in Peru had returned home, CMS were not prepared to send me there alone. They suggested I complete my studies and then they would decide where I was to serve. I couldn't believe it. God had brought me to St Andrews Hall and now the way to South America was blocked. I was again hopelessly confused and knew I just had to hold onto the belief that God was in control, and that "nothing is impossible" for him. I knew I had to let go of what I wanted—Peru—but somehow I couldn't.

Early in my time at St Andrew's Hall I clashed badly with some fellow students. Was this because of my uncertainty or just who I was? I wrote in my diary: "I feel crushed, Lord. I so much want to walk with you yet I have absolutely messed up. I need your forgiveness and your filling to start again in a new way." On Easter Sunday, I was reprimanded for getting a situation wrong. I reacted negatively, full of self-justification. Would I never learn? I often went for a walk after I felt I had messed up, and seeing the beauty of God's creation helped calm me down. I would go back to begin again, praying, "Please, God, transform me to be like Jesus."

Living together in such close community, along with the prayer time we had with one prayer partner each day, were as much part of our learning experience at St Andrew's Hall as the lectures. I valued my time praying with Margaret Lawry (later Brain). As we knelt together for the half hour after lunch in one of our bedrooms, time and time again she would pray for the very thing God had put on my heart. We saw many answers to our specific prayers, which was most encouraging.

At one stage one of my friends from Deaconess House, Lyn, gave me the task of keeping her growing relationship with one of the male students, Mike Perini, hidden. This was not always easy. Several times I had to answer "not sure" when I was asked where they were. I was relieved and thankful when they announced their engagement on 20

May. I wrote: "I long to express the joy, the wonder at God's fantastic work. Their news explodes within me, like the majesty of stars on a cloudless night, like the fragrance of a thousand roses, like the wonder of a baby's first cry. Enfold them in your love, Lord."

It was a few days before, on 12 May, that I had my one and only interview with the CMS Federal Candidates Committee. I was thrilled to hear that Scripture Union Peru had requested that a staff worker be sent. It seemed that God was opening the door for me to go there after all. My call to Peru was finally confirmed in June when I received a letter from CMS "offering" me a job in Peru working with Scripture Union in schools. I was stunned to realise that now, almost nineteen years later, the promise I had made at the age of eight to go to Peru was to become a reality.

I had two subjects to finish for my DipTh and then I would leave for South America. The official invitation came on 1 September 1975, from Paul Clark, Regional Secretary for Scripture Union in the Americas.

> I am glad to inform you that the Board unanimously voted to extend to you a warm invitation to come to this land to serve Jesus Christ under the auspices of Scripture Union … At this moment we are undergoing some major changes and it is marvellous to see how once again God is providing just what we need. Due to my increased responsibilities at the Regional level, I have resigned from the Peruvian movement, this resignation effective from 1 July 1976. In all probability I will be replaced by an entirely Spanish-speaking man which gives us concern for several aspects of the work, which demands a bilingual person. We are now praying you will fill this important spot … Let me say here that your work would lie particularly in the area of schools work and holiday activities, particularly camping.

I was so aware that God had prepared me for this role, and so excited, that I couldn't stop talking to all my St Andrew's Hall friends about it. I went on and on about having to learn Spanish and learn about Peruvian culture, wondering how long that would take and where I would study. At one point Bishop Stanway, the acting principal, looked at me and said, "Young lady, it's not what you do in a hundred years that counts. It's who you are moment by moment." I felt rebuked, but I have never forgotten this important truth. I prayed, "Help me please, Father, to learn *to be*."

I felt so thankful that I finally knew I was going to Lima, but I still did not know when. When my appointment was announced publicly on 5 October, I still had no idea when I was to leave. I felt frustrated, so I wrote to CMS asking for news. My friends at college supported me through this further time of uncertainty. On 23 October I wrote in my diary:

> Fellowship, friends in abundance, Lord, that's what
> you've given me. People who care, whose love abides,
> made perfect in Jesus crucified. They give of themselves,
> not counting the cost, sacrifice, not looking for gain.
> Pour your abundance, Lord, on them, your blessings
> over and over again. Cleanse me from my pride,
> which hinders what use I can be. Deliver me from the
> attraction of self, centre the glory on you.

I heard later that CMS had written to Paul Clark on 23 October expressing concern that they had not heard from him since August. They asked what plans Scripture Union had for when I was to leave and inquired about what I should take with me, where I would learn the language, where I would live and the best bank to open an account with so that payments of my allowance would be straightforward.

Meanwhile, my friend Barbara was shattered by unexpected and much unwanted news concerning a relationship. I wrote to her:

> To enfold you with arms of comfort, my friend,
> to ease the burden you bear,
> to protect you from the onslaught within,
> to defeat the despair.
> The yearning is there but not the right,
> it's the Cross you are chosen to bear.

> The path will be rough and fraught with sharp stones
> but I know He will meet you there.
> Joy there will be in your dark days of pain,
> comfort for all your fears.
> He *will* meet you at your moment of need
> Trust all to his perfect care.

I needed that message myself.

Exams over, I finished my second year at St Andrew's Hall, still not knowing when I was to leave for Peru. CMS were keen to send me as soon as possible, but when a reply came from Paul Clark in November, he said I should not come until after 7 May 1976. He would not be in the country until that date and wanted to meet me, explaining, "It is our intention to take her under our wing." He asked for my complete name and my mother's maiden name, and said the Concilio Nacional Evangélico del Perú (CONEP, the legal entity representing Protestant Christian organisations in Peru) would arrange my entry visa and notify the Peruvian consulate in Sydney. My visa could then be stamped into my passport. He concluded, "There is a big job waiting for her and she will want to work her way into it slowly … we look forward to taking the very best care of her."

CMS wrote to Paul expressing disappointment that I could not leave earlier. I was more than disappointed. I felt devastated. I wrote:

> Give me peace in the valley of despair
> Give me trust in your power and in your care
> Give me confidence, I pray, in your promises today
> Help me, Lord, to praise you now and evermore.
> Teach me, Lord, teach me, Lord, how to pray
> How to come in the name of Jesus Christ our King
> You have said to ask of you, you will give to all who do
> Teach me, Lord, teach me Lord, how to pray.
>
> Alleluia, alleluia, praise you, Lord
> Praise the Father, praise the Son
> Praise the Spirit, three in one
> Alleluia, praise the risen Lord of all.

The Queensland Times

IPSWICH, TUESDAY, MAY 25, 1976. *Recommended Price* 10c

MODERN DAY MISSIONARY HEADS FOR PERU

A YOUNG Ipswich woman, who has never been out of Australia before, is preparing to spend the next three years in Peru.

She is Miss Lesley McGrath of Bedford St., a primary teacher, who is going to Lima, the Peruvian capital as a missionary with the Anglican Church Missionary Society.

For many years Lesley has organised weekend and holiday camps for schoolchildren and this experience will assist her in her work.

She will be helping orphaned youth while in Peru.

"Some will be retired parents, others solely people," she said.

"In Peru, there is much more emphasis on providing the needs of the poorer people, and the issue of this charge will be of direct use to the underprivileged people.

"I will be very much involved with supervising these and helping them. Personal matters sharing the gospel.

"In effect I shall be working myself out of a job by training others to follow on and then I shall stop there."

Lesley said during to deport for an idea of the second summer.

"Missionaries are longer received in community by 1900s any way," she explained.

"They place over half to the fences have now shifting on to others.

She will be learning Spanish a week on Wednesday and in due two living with a Peruvian family for the better to get Spanish quicker. The people now talk at least some small and a special say what has to dated to check out to chance to settle out."

She will be working directly under the Peruvian general council at the Peruvian Union.

She admits to a few horses wobbles about the commitment shout the next three years in Peru.

But I realise that is an control and has guided me life so far and will continue to do so. she said.

"I am not going with the idea of helping a have been in Australia, because I am only have to their because I know I would be more success looking after the folds but as the middle of the road people so far just my own feeling states had the rest."

"I have been drawn in my missionary work for a long time.

"As a commented Christian I see the best to make a useful ground by sharing my own with a fresh new try.

As a governess, for the last started for with four the past three years in Brisbane and Melbourne.

Diplomas in Theology.

A relaxation course will be held by one of his Co-op Christian in the UK up to fly the French before he leaves.

● Leatey McGrath is going on a mission is a many to Peru next week, on top of the last period or from to which she has picked her promising staff for her leaving.

RATES UP AGAIN?

Shortfall in Federal allocation

IPSWICH ratepayers could face a paralysing increase in rates next year and the Ipswich City Council will be powerless to do anything about it.

Increased rates forced on the council by inflated costs and materials will climb another 5 percent because of Federal Government cutbacks in local government allocations.

Local government sources told in Canberra yesterday that rates would be increased by about 15 percent of total income.

That said if new works based increases of about 5 and programmes were required by ratepayers to permit. If any programmes their shares or municipalities, rates would have to be increased further.

The Australian Council of Local Government Associations met in Canberra yesterday and held talks with the Prime Minister, Mr. Fraser and the Minister assisting him in Federalist matters, Senator Carrick.

President of the association, Cr. W. J. Thwaites of Victoria, said: At a Press conference today an issue and been received at the meeting with Mr. Fraser, that future Government support under the Federation scheme would not fall below the levels reached in the last three years under the Labor Government.

Support

Local Government asked for 5 percent of the amount going to the States under the new Federalism policy but the Treasurer Mr. Lynch answered a few Thursday that local government would receive $146 million or about 1.8 per cent.

The 1 percent level would make up about 25 percent of total local government revenue, while the 1.8 percent makes up about 15 percent of total income.

Therefore an across-the-board increase of about 5 percent in rates was expected for the Department of Environment, Housing and Community Development which amounted to $100 million.

All governments according to Cr. Thwaites, will also affected by the Federal Government sending out of the Australian Assistance Plan, and Cr. Thwaites said it would be up to the State Governments to decide whether or not they supported the scheme.

Affected

Local government asked Senator Carrick and Mr. Fraser to provide details of Government spending cuts.

Local governments are also affected by the $100 Federal Government spending out of the Australian Assistance Plan, and Cr. Thwaites said it would be up to the State Governments to decide whether or not they supported the scheme.

Details of local road programmes were still to be announced by the Transport Minister, Mr. Nixon, he added.

McGRATH SCRIPTURE UNION CALLAO PERU SOUTH AMERICA

BLAIR BURIAL AT PURGA?

BRISBANE — The final resting place of little-known aboriginal hero, Harold Blair, is expected to be the Purga mission cemetery near Ipswich.

The funeral will be held in Melbourne today.

However a family of the deceased knows and probably first of Mr. Blair's best wishes has been for his ashes to be welcomed to the aborigines of the Purga mission where he spent much of his time.

NO SGIO PROBE

BRISBANE — The State Treasurer and Parliamentary Liberal Leader, Sir Gordon Chalk, last night rejected a move for an inquiry into the State Government Insurance Office.

Sir Gordon said he could see no sound reason for an inquiry into the SGIO.

He said the SGIO which paid its tax to the Federal Government had paid $20 million in support last to State Government hope in the last eight years.

Sir Gordon, Ministerial head of the SGIO said in the of the most extensive statement on the operations, has one set of Government funds went into the office.

He said he would fight against any major changes in the operation of the SGIO.

He said, generally, its investments and been successful.

It has not exercised the charter and had not undertaken any activity which had not already been engaged in by the underwriters.

The National Party State president, Mr. R. L. Sparkes, is seeking the inquiry. Mr. Sparkes said yesterday he would ask the National Party's management committee next Monday to consider allowing for a Parliamentary inquiry into the SGIO.

INSIDE TODAY

P.3 Commuters ready.
P.4 Hayden on the law
P.5 Uranium issue
P.9 Health to cost $10

Features				
	P.4 TV. Comics	P.10
Editorial	P.6 Classified	P.17
Women	P.11 Finance	P.21
Country	P.15 Sport	P.22

FORECAST: Fine, mod. winds. Max. 24 degrees.

THIS WEEK'S R.T. EDWARDS ELECTRICAL SPECIALS

Booval Shopping Centre and 66 EAST STREET, IPSWICH 281 4133

SANYO Kerosene Heater	DOUBLE BED Dual Control Electric Blankets	1000 WATT Single Bar Radiator
$39.95	$19.95	$6.95

COLOUR TV AND SERVICE EXPERTS!

TEN

Perfect timing

Knowing I was not leaving until May, I decided to visit Karen in Adelaide and see my niece Melanie and her new-born sister, Stephanie. I also went to Townsville and Cairns to visit my North Queensland friends, who promised to support me in prayer. It was good to have time at home in Booval with the family and to be able to join again in the church life at All Saints. I began to see how God's timing was perfect. I wrote: "Thank you for the precious time you have provided … time with friends so perfect, the sense of fellowship tremendous."

As I was going as a Queensland missionary, John Arnold, the CMS Queensland General Secretary, and I arranged my commissioning service to be held at All Saints Booval on 30 May 1976. The Revd Jim Holbeck, whom I knew from Youth Fellowship days, was asked to preach. During May, the CMS Federal Secretary, Maurice Betteridge, wrote confirming I would leave from Sydney on 4 June flying first to New Zealand where I would join a flight to Papeete, Tahiti. From there I would change to an Air France plane to head for Lima, arriving on 5 June. I was told I would be met at Lima.

At this stage, decisions as to my allowance had not been made. CMS and SU Peru—or Unión Bíblica, as Scripture Union is known throughout South America—were to share the cost of my serving. I was told, though, that my allowance would be remitted monthly, with an initial three-month payment to help me settle in and learn the language. I was to go to the Pontifical Catholic University in Lima for two hours of classes a week, plus an hour of language laboratory. I was to "lend a hand" at an English-speaking Unión Bíblica Young People's meeting on Friday nights and give "a little help with correspondence in English" at the Unión Bíblica office. I was given no definite details about accommodation, but the hope was that I could "stay for the first few weeks with an English-speaking family, probably Paul and Marty Clark".

At home in early May, I started thinking about what I should take with me. I could only take two suitcases on the plane, so I managed to acquire a couple of large blue forty-four-gallon drums on which a signwriter friend kindly painted my name and destination. Deciding what I needed and packing it became a big, rushed job. The drums were ultimately stuffed with an unbreakable dinner set, a bedspread and sheets, towels, kitchenware and much more. They were to be collected and shipped to Lima.

Ipswich's daily newspaper, *The Queensland Times*, heard about my going and sent a reporter and photographer to our home to interview me. My story became front-page news.

> A young Ipswich woman who has never been out of Australia before is preparing to spend the next three years in Peru … She will be helping organise youth camps. "Some will be travel camps, others study camps," she says. "In Peru there is much more emphasis on involving youth of the country in social service, and some of the camps will be of direct aid to underprivileged people. I will be helping to train Peruvian leaders." … She admits to a few human qualms about her commitment to spend the next three years in Peru. "But I believe God is in control and has guided my life so far, and will continue to do so … As a committed Christian I saw the need to totally commit myself by sharing my life a long time ago."

Yes, I did have those qualms. On 25 April I wrote:

> I'm alone—so alone—and not understood,
>   a barrier within.
> Did you feel alone, misunderstood?
> I look to you, Lord, and speak of the cost,
> Tell of the barrier you crossed,
> Ignoring the cost to open the gate.

Your example in giving, not looking to take,
is what I see in your word.
I've shared it with others all over the place.
I've lost sight of your wonderful face.
The words I've said re-echo in my ears.
How dare I stand and proclaim,
Speak out and share when I only know turmoil,
   unrest within?
And now the doubts flood in, overwhelming my mind.
Why must the doubt and fears be there?
Jesus alone understands all I fear.
Make me aware of your presence always.

Dad's birthday was on 29 May, and I was aware that it was the last occasion for a very long time when I would be with my family. We celebrated Toni's birthday, 7 June, on the same day so I could be there. Toni was now married and expecting her first child in July. I would not be there to greet my next niece or nephew. I cried out, "Father, bless my family and care for them please."

The commissioning service was wonderful. The psalm I chose was Psalm 27. I asked that verse 10—"Though my father and mother forsake me, the Lord will receive me"—be left out; I didn't want Mum to be offended. Dad and my brother Ian read the lessons with conviction. I promised myself that I would keep praying specially for fifteen-year-old Ian. Jim Holbeck preached on 2 Corinthians 5, urging me to be "an ambassador for Christ" as I went, and as those I left behind prayed. The final hymn declared, "How firm a foundation, ye saints of the Lord, is laid for your faith in his excellent word … 'Fear not, I am with thee, O be not dismayed.'" These words stayed with me long after the service, and this is still one of my favourite songs.

The day of my departure, 3 June, arrived, and as Dad got the car out I was still jamming things into my suitcases. Mum, Dad, Ian, Debra and Andrew were seeing me off from Brisbane airport. About twenty minutes on our way I suddenly shouted in horror, "My ticket! I've left it at home!" After a few minutes of frenzied searching, Dad and I left Mum and Ian at Oxley with instructions to ring our neighbour,

Mrs Wallis, and ask her to go into our house and search for the ticket. "It's all right, Lesley," Ian said, "maybe the plane will be hijacked!" Dad drove as fast as he safely could while I prayed madly. Mrs Wallis was waiting with the ticket. We raced back, picked up Mum and Ian and made it to the plane. I arrived in Sydney frazzled but on time.

I lunched next day with Maurice Betteridge and had tea at night with Felicity Fries. She took me to the airport and we booked one of my suitcases and my guitar through.

The next day, friends and CMS folk came to see me off. Once through to the duty-free section, I impetuously bought a wind-up koala that played *Waltzing Matilda*. I wanted something tangible to remember this moment. It was a source of amusement to young Peruvians who visited my apartment, and even today it helps me remember that farewell moment.

I had never travelled overseas before and was so excited. In my diary I wrote: "I am on my way … How can I express the joy and privilege? Now all is so radically new … Words fail me, yet I know of your love shown through my friends. Grow me to know and express your love in all I am. Make me *your* ambassador, please, in Peru."

In Auckland I was told my flight to Tahiti had been cancelled and I was to catch an Air New Zealand flight instead. It left at 1 am. I was able to help an Argentine couple who spoke only Spanish to understand the change. Through meeting them I realised, probably for the first time, that it was not only the language but also the culture that I would need to learn in order to live and work in Peru.

It was 3.35 am Sydney time when we reached Papeete. The four-hour stopover gave me only a glimpse of Tahiti's blue coral cay, towering peaks and deep ravines. I was so tired that once we'd arrived at a hotel, I ate a quick and, for me, small breakfast, went straight to bed and slept. I later found I could have eaten a much better breakfast; the cost was included in my ticket! Confusingly, having crossed the International Date Line, I found it was still 4 June when I boarded the Air France flight to Lima. On this leg of the journey, I was at times overwhelmed with thrill and terror. I prayed, "Lord, now is the chance to prove your greatness and your power: fill me with your love. Teach me to trust you fully. Make me adaptable and sensitive." I was incredibly tired.

When we touched down in Lima, I calculated it was 5 am Lima time on Saturday 5 June 1976.

Paul and Marty Clark and their children: Billie, Johnny and Janie.
1976

ELEVEN

The scent of Peru

I shall never forget the smell of my early arrival in Lima. It was like a stale cattle yard. How thankful I was to hear my name called from the open terminal rooftop as I disembarked! Someone was there to meet me.

There were in fact four early risers waiting—John MacPherson from the Unión Bíblica board; Mariano Lint, the Camps Committee chairman; Petronio Allauca, the new Unión Bíblica Peru General Secretary; and Bishop Bill Flagg from the Anglican Church. Lima airport was cold and primitive in comparison to the other airports I had been through, and I was so thankful when Bishop Flagg arranged to help me through customs. Nothing incurred charges, and to my joy I found my guitar, which I had booked through from Sydney, was there for me to collect. Customs took less than an hour, and John explained that we were all going to his place for breakfast. He said he hoped Paul Clark, the only one in Peru with whom I had been in contact, would be there too. They were surprised he had not arrived at the airport.

We had finished breakfast before Paul arrived. He apologised, explaining that the road between Lima and Chaclacayo, where he lived, had been blocked by huge rocks. Four thousand factory workers were on strike and they had taken to the roads, hurling rocks. I was immediately thrown into the uncertain reality of Peruvian life. It was planned that I would stay with Paul and his family for a month, by which time it was hoped I would be able to board with a Peruvian family.

Our thirty-two-kilometre drive from Lima to Chaclacayo was on the road to the Andes. Up and up we drove, and all I saw were barren hills, sandy brown dirt and not one blade of grass. By the time we arrived at Paul's home, a lovely two-storey mudbrick house, I was exhausted.

I met Marty, Paul's wife, and their children, Janie, Billie and Johnny. Then I collapsed and slept for over three hours. My lovely room, their guest room, had a parquet floor and an en-suite, with a view of their green walled garden and the bare brown hills beyond. This was not the sort of accommodation I was expecting. I learned later that the water for their home came from the Rímac River, fed by snow from the Andes. It was distributed from an open aqueduct. The line of this ditch was green and very clear to see across the brown landscape.

It was almost 5 pm when I woke up. Afternoon tea was being served, and John MacPherson and his wife, Catherine, had popped in to visit. As we talked, I realised this meal was equivalent to our "dinner" back home. I was not sorry to return to my room to sleep quite early. The trip had drained me.

The next day was Sunday, so I went to an Iglesia Evangélica Peruana service with the Clark family. The church was in a poor district only a few kilometres from their home. It was a painted cement building right on the street and looked the same as all the other buildings around it. The pastor met us and showed us around, then started the service. I watched as a young mother quite naturally lifted her baby from her back and breastfed him. The noise of loud music and street vendors outside made it hard to hear the message, and the obvious poverty disturbed me when I thought of the affluence of our Australian churches.

As we left the church, I heard what sounded like loud firecrackers. It turned out to be the music of a small procession, led by someone carrying a cross, moving down the street. I was to see many such processions over the years.

Marty bought some fruit at a stall and we set off back to Chaclacayo. The roads were packed with slow-moving cars heading for the mountains. "Smog, caused by car fumes, is like a giant blanket covering the city, so on weekends people head for the mountains to find the sun," Paul explained.

When we arrived home, we found Marty's maid was very unwell, so we drove her up the hillside to the closest nurse. The nurse lived in a small neat house, meticulously clean in spite of the dirt and dust everywhere. She diagnosed the early stages of pneumonia, so it was home to bed for the maid. Visitors came for tea, and Marty served waffles. I discovered meat was a luxury and very expensive. So far I had only had it once—thin "hot dogs".

On Monday Marty took me to Chosica on a *micro* bus, giving me my first experience of Peruvian markets. Soon after arriving we heard a band playing, and again I saw a large crowd paying homage to a huge statue of the crucified Christ. I felt the superstition and lack of real understanding among the people and was overcome with sorrow for them. Marty told me their fiesta would continue into the night with firecrackers and drunkenness.

I wandered around the market stalls in amazement at the array of goods on offer. There were many varieties of fruit and vegetables, some, such as the granadilla, new to me. I was surprised to see that prices for luxury items were similar to prices in Australia. Few Peruvians would be able to afford much that Australians took for granted. Marty bought a floor polisher and a vacuum cleaner, and I spent three hours vacuuming the house when we got home. I recognised how pressured Marty would be without her maid—everything in Peru seemed to take much longer than in Australia.

When Paul and the children came home from school that afternoon, we went for a swim at a local club, El Bosque, where they were members. I was conscious that this was a luxury only middle-class families could afford. I spent as much time as possible during that first week listening to the radio so I could get used to Spanish. I also wrote my first letter home to the family. I missed them all so much, and I was anxiously awaiting news of Toni's baby.

We did not go back to the Iglesia Evangélica Peruana the next Sunday but attended a Brethren church in Chosica. The Clarks were checking out churches to see if there was one nearer to home that would suit their family. Although we were made welcome, they decided this one did not meet their criteria either.

On my second Monday in the country, Paul took me in to Lima to collect my unaccompanied suitcase from the airport, help me open a bank account and find out about Spanish classes. I was also keen to post my letter. Collecting my suitcase turned into a marathon effort. We had to visit numerous officers and sign many papers before it was released—I feared I would have to spend the whole day at the airport. In the end, though, we did have time to open a bank account, and discovered that we were a day early for enrolling in language classes at the university.

Marty kindly came with me by bus next day to show me the route to the Catholic University and help me enrol. Classes were to start the following day, and I was to travel alone. Marty warned me not to take too much cash with me, so I put 100 soles in my bra and only a small amount in my purse. My fare was nine soles. I was again surprised to see a young mother, who looked about sixteen and had a three-year-old boy, unselfconsciously breastfeeding her baby. I had to get off the bus at the terminus, so that part was easy.

The university was about fifteen minutes' walk away. I wandered through a market. The fruit looked tempting, but as all the food was exposed to the open air, I didn't dare buy anything. All manhole covers in Peru seemed to have been stolen and I had to keep a watch so I didn't fall into one. The traffic too was mad. Peruvian drivers seemed to drive by instinct rather than any rules, and I had to remember to look to the left, right and left again—the opposite to our Australian way.

When I arrived at the Plaza San Martin, I went into the Hotel Bolivar to go to their bathroom. Looking foreign and middle class, I could do this without anyone questioning me, though it was not a place many of the Peruvian friends I made later would have been able to enter. I paid two soles for six squares of toilet paper. This was the only toilet I ever knew of in the centre of Lima.

At the university I attended my first classes, which lasted about an hour and a half. Re-entering the Plaza, I saw a vendor I had noticed before, so I decided to buy some peanuts. Somehow, as I made my purchase, my purse disappeared. I was so thankful for Marty's warning. I had the money for my bus fare home in my bra. The stolen purse had been a gift from a friend so I felt sad to lose it.

Two days of travelling to and from classes and a reception to welcome me to Peru on the Thursday night left me on Friday feeling overwhelmed and very tired. I understood little at the welcome party but appreciated the beautiful roses they presented to me, a symbol of love. Hardly anyone spoke in English, and I even found it hard to reproduce the few Spanish words I'd learnt. I wondered when I would be able to communicate properly. I wrote later:

> Can you use me, Lord, this vessel that you made?
> It seems just so impossible, this life is still just clay.
> How can others see your Son shown forth in me
>   since my imperfections abound?
> Teach me, Lord, to wait your time,
>   to keep in touch with you,
> That though imperfect I am still, others will see just you.

On Sunday I was taken to a session of an InterVarsity Fellowship (IVF) conference where I met Samuel and Lily Escobar, who later became close friends.

How wonderful it was to receive a letter from Dad! He told me that he and Toni's husband, Gary, had taken my forty-four-gallon drums to be shipped to me. He concluded the letter with the words, "Sorry for the scrawl. If you can't read it, send it back and I'll write it again." I laughed. Two days later Dad wrote again saying they had received my first letter and everyone had been excited to hear from me. It had been read to the Brisbane Synod, the CMS General Committee and, of course, to many at All Saints Booval. "It is encouraging to see the love and concern from the whole community," he wrote. I felt loved and cared for in my aloneness.

On the day of my visa medical appointment, I went into the centre of Lima and walked about five kilometres, visiting four plazas. I began to get a glimpse into this city of four million people. I had been told there was a growing middle class, but many of the people I saw would have lived in homes with no running water. My medical appointment was a frightening experience. The doctor stepped over the line, and I hadn't the language to stop him. I felt contaminated and prayed for the Lord to cleanse me and fill me. I felt so useless, struggling as I was with the language.

I was keen to explore the Plaza de Armas, the oldest public square in Peru. It was designated as the city centre by the conquistador Francisco Pizarro in 1535, and the key administrative and commercial buildings surrounded it. Every city in Peru has a Plaza de Armas as its centre.

The cathedral was there, and I was amazed to see the abundance of gold, crystal and silver inside. I watched people praying to the many images around, all of which had an offertory box beside them. There were stalls selling religious paraphernalia. I was struck by the emphasis on the suffering of Christ and wondered if it reflected the poverty of so many Peruvians.

Back outside in the plaza, I walked towards the Palacio de Gobierno, the sixteenth-century home of Peru's president. I admired the guards in their stunning white and red uniforms. The Palacio Municipal was the town hall and council chambers and the Palacio de la Unión housed Union Club. The word *palacio* means "palace" and these were indeed very palatial and majestic old buildings. The houses around them had belonged to the wealthy in the sixteenth century. Some had intricately carved wooden balconies—I was told that these were built so ladies could look down, unobserved, and watch the markets, bull-fights and city gallows. Many died during the Inquisition, and my later visit to the museum was a gruesome experience filled with the instruments of torture used on those accused of heresy.

In the following weeks I faced several problems that were new to me. Two things that really got to me were the attitude of many Peruvian men and the rule that you literally threw anything you didn't want on the ground. I did not like the looks many men gave me when I went into Lima and the fact that some deliberately touched me as I passed. There was also social turmoil in the city—the Peruvian currency was devalued, prices rose and the people reacted. Inflation hit the poor hard. There were riots in the city, and the government declared a state of emergency, imposing a curfew. Anyone outside between 10 pm and 5 am would be shot on sight. Seeing military personnel with sub-machineguns and police with revolvers soon became the norm. I had two whole weeks without classes and was concerned that my language learning was badly slowed down.

Paul and Marty felt I would be ready to move into a Peruvian home where I would not be able to speak English by 1 August. They suggested they take me for an orientation trip on the Andes train before that date, and they would have a short family holiday doing this. They arranged for me to briefly meet the Señora I would stay with before I moved in. I was thankful to find she was a middle-class woman and her home had a bathroom with hot and cold water. I was to stay with her and her husband for a month on a trial basis.

I had taken some time to adjust to Marty's American cooking—we had mashed potatoes with marshmallows on top! My stomach reacted to different foods as well as to the water. I wondered how I would manage with just a Peruvian diet, which I was told was mostly noodles, rice and spicy foods. Few could afford much meat or cheese. I was thankful that I would begin to eat Peruvian food on our trip before moving house. This would be the beginning of my next stage of cultural and language learning.

Fruit stall outside the church.
1976

TWELVE

Language and culture

I had another week of language school before we went on our holiday. During that time I stayed for a couple of days with the MacPherson family who had been at the airport to meet me. Dr Leon Morris and his wife, Mildred, were visiting them. I felt privileged to meet this renowned Bible teacher. The MacPhersons remembered that it was my birthday on 18 July and gave me a writing pad. To my great joy, I received a cable from my Booval church with a few words added by Dad and Mum. Then, when I went into Lima to the post office, I found a letter from Dad and a card from the family.

Another joy to me was to be notified that my drums of household goods had reached the port of Lima and that a fellow from CONEP would arrange for them to be stored until I had a place of my own. I was relieved not to have to collect them myself. I already had so many new experiences and people to adjust to, and on top of this I was struggling to learn the language and understand the many differences in the way things were done in Peru. At times I felt completely inadequate.

Even paying for things in shops was new and complicated. In markets we simply paid and received our goods and change. But in shops the buyer received a docket, took it to a cashier who wrote another docket when the goods were paid for, and then took this second docket to the collection section to pick up the parcel. I constantly prayed for patience and the ability to learn and fit in.

The night before we left for our holiday, I woke feeling a strange sensation as if the earth was shaking. It was! This, my first earth tremor, only lasted a short time. On our way to the railway station next morning, Paul asked me if I had felt the earthquake. "That was only a small one," he said. "Usually when you feel shaking, you should immediately go outside or get under a table."

We'd left very early for the station because we knew we would have to queue up to board the train. Paul had bought first-class tickets but was unable to reserve seats. We arrived and stood in our first queue outside the station. At 6 am a gate was opened slightly so that those with tickets could form new queues in the foyer. After half an hour or so we were allowed through another door, which we thought would take us to the platform—but no, it was our next queue-forming area. Official booking of seats did not open until 8 am, and even though the station master was there, he waited till then. There was a huge rush of people trying to get seats, but the train arrived before we could book. We joined the avalanche of people racing for it and scrambling to find seats. The first carriage we leapt into was packed, and in the second one we found seats but not together. Then for some reason the carriage suddenly emptied, and we were able to sit together.

The trip to Huancayo, one of the largest towns in the Andes, was unlike anything I had experienced before. It was 10 am when we finally got under way. The engine was at the front of the train for an hour or so, then we stopped at a siding while it was transferred to the back to push us. I lost count of the number of times this happened. We zigzagged up the mountain. At 3000 metres I saw glimpses of snow in the distance. We passed graveyards—mountain people didn't bury their dead but stacked the coffins, six high, in a wall. When earthquakes occurred, I was told, the walls would collapse and the coffins fall and split open. I saw llamas grazing or working like pack horses, and young shepherds caring for small flocks of sheep.

We reached the highest peak (4834 metres) at 2 pm. We all kept very still because moving could cause *soroche* (altitude sickness). Gradually we dropped down to 3600 metres and stopped at the town of La Oryora, where many joined the train for the four-hour trip to Huancayo. Large numbers had to stand for the whole journey. I nursed a small child, and we squashed up to let a seventy-five-year-old sit with us. A heavily pregnant woman was heading for the nearest hospital. Her contractions started and we wondered if she would make it.

We were exhausted when we arrived at Huancayo and headed straight to our hotel and bed. I had a cold and found breathing difficult. The next day we headed to the famous markets. I spent about

2000 soles (AUD$21) on an alpaca poncho with embroidered llamas, an alpaca cardigan and a wooden spoon with a painting on it.

Originally Quechua was the language of this town but gradually Spanish had taken over. Local arts and crafts were traded in the shops and markets, alongside modern factory-made goods. Although Huancayo was only eleven degrees south of the equator, the temperature was not hot because we were so high. In fact, at times I found myself quite cold.

The next day we went in a *colectivo*, a long-distance taxi, to Tarma, a beautiful mountain town in the Central Sierra about 3000 metres above sea level. After a few hours exploring the town, we took another taxi to La Merced, where the government had taken over a former Unión Bíblica campsite in the jungle named "Kimo". The purpose of this excursion was to look at land for sale that might become a new jungle campsite. The trip to La Merced was terrifying. My heart was in my mouth as we wove our way down 2100 metres. Sheer drops of hundreds of feet greeted us as we rounded many of the sharp curves. There were no protective barriers to prevent cars going over the side, and we passed many crosses reminding us of the lethal journey we were on.

Despite the danger, the scenery was spectacular. Hills rose thousands of metres into the air and wild orchids flourished in abundance. Dust flew up over everything. When we arrived at La Merced, I found that even my black bag in the boot was thick with dust.

La Merced is called "the eyebrow of the jungle" because it is the meeting point of the jungle and the mountain. Once settled into our hotel, we spent the next three hours trying to phone Paul's mother to check on her and the children. Once we got through, Mrs Clark senior told me she had received a cable from Australia to tell me that Toni's baby girl had arrived safely. My new niece was named Kirsty Jane. I was very excited and longed to be home to meet this precious new family member.

Our day in La Merced was 28 July, Peru's national day, so the town was in a celebratory mood. We went to the Plaza de Armas. Every building was flying the red-white-red Peruvian flag (they were fined if they didn't) and a band was playing—not quite in tune, but everyone enjoyed listening anyway. There were women from the Sierra in colourful dress carrying babies or produce on their backs, Indians in their mu-mu style clothing and everyone in between.

After a night in a clean room but a very smelly environment and a breakfast of fried bananas and coffee, we set off to look for a new Kimo campsite. We travelled on the backs of several trucks, most of which had very little suspension. We were impressed with one block we saw. It had a beautiful view of the Chanchamayo River, two small streams, many fruit and avocado trees, and a large flat area where we could build. It was on the opposite side of the river to the road, so campers would have to cross by huaro (cable car), which was really a platform hauled across the fast-flowing river. It carried a maximum of six people. I knew it would take a lot of negotiating for us to buy this property, so I left Paul to do the talking and prayed.

As we made the perilous eight- or nine-hour trip back to Lima, I thought: If Paul succeeds in buying the block, this is the road we will have to travel on for Kimo camps. The road was narrow, and when we met trucks coming in the opposite direction, we had to back up to let them pass. I was more than apprehensive. I did, however, find it an incredible experience to go from steamy jungle, up steep roads into the Andes again, then back down to the arid coast and Lima.

On 1 August, two days after arriving back, I moved into my new Peruvian home. I saw very little of the Señora and her husband. I suspected that, since they had never had a boarder before, they felt unsure how to communicate with me. I practised my Spanish with the maid. The hours my hosts kept were so unusual that I usually ate by myself. They normally had their lunch between 4.30 and 5 pm, then dinner after 10 pm. I found the carbohydrate diet of rice with potato and sauce, or small bread rolls with sauce (sometimes containing a little chicken), hard to cope with.

Language study progressed slowly. I was not getting much practice at home and was very discouraged. I felt like a child again as I struggled with the position of nouns and pronouns relative to verbs. One day before class started, another of the students burst into tears. I felt like doing the same. I had such limited ability to speak a coherent sentence. Then it occurred to me that when Mariano Lint had rung to invite me to a folklore concert, I had actually understood him.

I had been asked to help with the Friday night English Bible studies and the Sunday night English Group activities at the Union Church. I wondered if this might affect my progress in Spanish but decided to accept the challenge anyway. To make sure my Spanish improved, I found, at 300 soles an hour, a private tutor named Gloria de Gross. I went to her twice a week from 6 to 7 pm. She gave me work to do at home such as summarising articles from *Selecciones (Reader's Digest)*, which we would then discuss. Gloria lived with her daughter in Lima but her husband lived in Arequipa. He evidently had a mistress there, but Gloria would not divorce him. Our conversations often lasted much longer than the hour I paid for.

I was struggling. On 10 September 1976, I wrote:

> Why this void of loneliness now,
> A deep throbbing ache within?
> Tear-filled with yearning for caring love
> To be a whole person again.
>
> Usefulness, security are but fleeting thought
> As the struggle suppressed surges on.
> Not one of us, Lord, can exist on our own
> I'm convinced of that within.
> Giving and receiving there has to be,
> Done in a selfless way.
> Reactions, attitudes tuned to *you*, Lord
> Seeking fulfilment from *you.*
>
> Satisfaction, fulfilment Jesus does give
> As I lay my needs before him.
> Lord God, I cast myself on your loving care
> Give me faith to trust that you are there!

I greatly enjoyed the night I spent at the folklore concert with Mariano, his fiancée, Margarita, and his sister Berenice. There were dances from the different regions of the Peruvian Andes and we had supper of *anticuchos*—pieces of marinated beef heart on skewers—followed by small doughy donuts in a sugary syrup. I felt happy and thought that maybe these people would meet my need for friendship (and indeed they did). They were patient teachers and I valued their introduction to Peruvian culture.

I found my efforts at travelling on *micros* less encouraging. The aim of these mini-vans or very small buses was to carry as many passengers as possible. The driver's helper hung out the door as it was moving and hopped down when it stopped so he could push people in. Many micros had such low roofs that when I had to stand (which was mostly), I had to stoop for the whole trip. The *colectivo* taxis were not much better, though certainly more expensive. They were ordinary cars that displayed a destination on the windscreen, and the owners picked up multiple customers and charged everyone the same amount. Trips often took a very long time.

Beggars were everywhere in and around Lima. Children used to hop onto the buses, sing a song or recite a ditty, and then ask all the passengers for money. I learnt that many were not really poverty-stricken, but of course some were. I had no way of judging which ones to help. I found it harder to accept the thieving. I learnt not to take anything I valued with me when I went out and to hold lightly to material possessions. They easily disappeared in a crowd.

During my time at the Señora's I had my second trip to La Merced. This was with members of the Unión Bíblica Camps Committee to inspect the possible new campsite. We left at 9 pm, and I gazed out at moonlit snow at about 2 am. We encountered a landslide, the first of many I would see in Peru. It was 1.30 pm next day when we finally reached La Merced. I was back on the bank of the Chanchamayo River. This time it was unexpectedly raining and we all got soaked. Crossing the river in the cable platform took longer than last time and was decidedly wetter. But the potential site was superb, and the owner was willing to sell. We just had to find the money.

I did not enjoy boarding and spent a lot of time and energy looking for an apartment of my own. I had only just arrived home when I got an urgent call from Paul to say that a friend of Marty's had an apartment in the Miraflores District of Lima she was prepared to rent to me.

THIRTEEN

A new home

As I had been looking for an apartment, I had prayed for one in a good location transport-wise, with a view and good airflow. The apartment Marty took me to had it all and was larger than I had hoped for. Better still was the rent, which I could afford. I was over the moon.

From the balcony, which overlooked a street lined with lovely deciduous trees, I could see the Pacific Ocean, only a short walk away. The apartment was on the third floor and had two bedrooms, a maid's room, a lounge/dining room big enough to hold a large group, and a decent-sized kitchen. There were three toilets, one in the bathroom, one in the maid's room and one in the hallway. I was not sure how useful a hallway toilet would be. I decided immediately that the maid's room would be my study. After two months with the Peruvian family, I was delighted to hear that I could move in at the end of the week.

I had a very busy time setting up the apartment as inexpensively as possible. I slept for two weeks on a camp stretcher while I searched for a reasonably priced bed base and mattress. There were no light fittings or curtains; I opted for basic light fittings like most people had, and I bought nine metres of beige hessian, covered with huge blue flowers, for the bedroom curtains. Friends kindly helped with sewing them and putting them up on rods. It did not take me long to realise I needed to buy a decent gas oven because the apartment only had cooktops.

The parquet floors needed a lot of upkeep and I knew I couldn't keep borrowing Marty's polisher. One of her male helpers came several times and did the first few polishes. It took him three hours to cover the whole apartment, so I decided to buy my own polisher and employ a maid one day a week. I found a young single mother with a son at school who was prepared to work for a foreigner. Her name was Gilda, and she proved to be all I could wish for. She came on Fridays. I gave her a key, and when I returned home from work at Unión Bíblica on Friday nights, I would walk into a fresh clean unit that smelt of polish and looked beautiful. I had bought pot plants to fill up spare corners and they were freshly watered. Gilda cleaned for me every week for all the years I was in Peru.

This amazing apartment was in an ideal location. I enjoyed the twenty-minute, seven-block walk to the supermarket. There was also a good "corner shop" close by if I needed something in a hurry. Getting to work was easy as I was on a direct *micro* route to the office. The centre of Miraflores was quite close, and from there I could catch buses to most parts of Peru.

I could not believe God's amazing provision. I wrote: "O my God, you have given in such a super abundant way. What do I lack? Nothing! This home to live in, to use in your service. Please, may your Spirit always dwell here. Keep me conscious of your provision always."

On 1 October I experienced two hours of sunshine. I noticed people's moods beginning to lift. They were starting to feel excited about summer coming! I was particularly looking forward to my first summer, when I would be responsible for twenty-seven camps from the end of December to the end of March 1977. I was to direct two of these personally and planned to visit the others. All the administrative work was done by Petronio Allauca. Unión Bíblica charged more for the English-speaking camps so that the cost for the Spanish-speaking camps could be kept within Peruvians' means. I tried, unsuccessfully at first, to encourage some plans for following up campers after they went home.

My Spanish was improving, but I was conscious of not being able to respond quickly or adequately in discussions. Small and big cultural differences also troubled me. This made me doubt my ability to run the camps. I had no alternative; I simply had to trust Almighty God's enabling and protection. I had to go to (and pay for) several functions arranged by members of the Camps Committee so that I could "make helpful contacts". I became more and more tired. The effort involved in getting anywhere, having to stand on the crowded micros and speaking nothing but Spanish was exhausting, and made me decide to have a break and visit Paul and Marty for a day. I took my language teacher, Gloria, and two of her children with me.

One day, when I was feeling a little more confident, I invited a young lady I had met to lunch at 12.30 pm. I was ready at that time and concerned at her non-appearance. She finally arrived at 2 pm. I discovered that in Peru it is impolite to arrive at the time invited. I began to understand why I was often left to sit on my own in the front room of a house when I was invited to dinner. I tried to entertain once a week at least and enjoyed trying out the different fruits and vegetables that were available. I often had to go the supermarket several times as I had to carry everything home myself, and I started to see the value of owning a car.

I was told October was the time El Señor de los Milagros (The Lord of Miracles) "goes walking". A painting of the crucified Christ survived an earthquake in Lima in the seventeenth century and since then had been venerated. The annual religious procession was the largest in the world (and still is today). People believed that participating in the procession would save them from harm during earthquakes. Hundreds of thousands walked in the procession, which travelled down different roads on different days. Many wore purple all through October in honour of El Señor de los Milagros. On my way home from my language tutorial one day, my curiosity led me to watch the procession. I saw milling crowds stretching out to touch the painting. As the procession came close to me, I was caught up in it and carried along against my will. I frantically fought my way out. I felt I understood afresh why Zacchaeus climbed a tree when Jesus was passing.

October had some special treats for the people. My favourite was *turrón de Doña Pepa*, an extremely sweet biscuit/pastry dessert covered with sticky syrup and topped with large hundreds and thousands.

October was also the month to go to a bull fight. I was taken by Mariano, Margarita and Berenice. Everyone there was dressed in their finest clothes. I was amazed at the splendour and pomp of the parade of superbly attired picadors. I joined the crowd laughing loudly as the bull, reacting to being poked with lances and short spears, leapt over a low fence, causing people to scatter. Once the bull was returned to the ring, it was met by a magnificently dressed matador who, to cries from the crowd of *olé!*, stepped with such fluidity out of the way of the charging bull and finally killed it cleanly. I found the idea of killing for sport hard to agree with, but for me it was an amazing experience and another insight into Peruvian culture.

My three friends next took me to a cockfight. This was an experience I never wanted to repeat. We were seated in the front row overlooking a sandy pit below. There was much gambling on which of the roosters would win. I noticed the birds had sharp razor blades attached to their legs. It was horrible to watch, and after the first fight I spent the rest of the time with my eyes firmly shut.

In November 1976 I took eighteen English-speaking young people down for a camp at Kawai on the coast. The campsite was in the Mala Valley bordering the frigid Pacific Ocean. The camp was designed to help the young people discover what it meant to live as a Christian in their environment. From the campsite we walked to a pre-Inca graveyard where it was possible to find human bones in the sand.

Later in the month I was again at Kawai. This time I was with Paul Clark and Nigel Sylvester, the International Secretary of Scripture Union, who was visiting Peru. I had met him at a reception at Felix Calle's home; Felix was the chairman of the Unión Bíblica Council. It made me aware how deeply I was into Unión Bíblica work, both their schools and camping work, while still trying to learn Spanish.

In November I also attended Mariano and Margarita's wedding. In Peru there were two marriage ceremonies: first a civil ceremony, then a church wedding (followed by a reception). The church service was moving. It was conducted in German for Margarita's family and Spanish for the rest of us. The reception was virtually overflowing with food, all presented beautifully around a stunning swan carved from ice. When the time came to eat, I was shocked that everyone made a dive for the table, grabbing everything they could. Soon it was bare. I learnt a lesson for future weddings if I wanted to eat anything!

FOURTEEN

Working with Unión Bíblica

I had come to Peru primarily to do schools work but had found myself more and more caught up in camps. My friend Mariano, who so greatly helped me understand Peruvian culture, was the chairman of the Camps Committee. He was also a part-time art teacher at two different schools. He was quite a gifted artist himself, so I was pleased when he offered to illustrate my newsletters home. I asked my parents to send him 2.5-centimetre crayons so he could illustrate his Bible talks at camps and schools. Several other members of the committee were also teachers, and I hoped these contacts would give me an opportunity to get involved in Unión Bíblica work in Peruvian schools.

Our tents at Kawai campsite were very dilapidated, so we were thrilled to receive a pile of new tents from Holland. They arrived the day before the first camp in December, so in one day we had to learn to put them up. The instructions were in poor Spanish, but somehow, after much trial and error, we discovered how they were meant to work.

Because I was to visit all the camps, I knew I needed a driver's licence. I was told I could use Petronio's car for this. Getting the licence was quite a process. First I had to do a twenty-question theoretical exam. I asked for and was given a translator. He found it difficult to read the questions to me in English, so he read them in Spanish and told me the answers in English. We scored nineteen out of twenty! I did not need to take the practical test. My Australian licence was looked at, then I was told to stand on one leg with my eyes closed for twenty seconds. With that I passed.

Because my apartment was so big and central, Mariano organised for most camp meetings to be held at my place. I also began to invite more people for dinner, and having grown up in a large family, I did not find catering for six to ten guests hard. It was the shopping and getting things to prepare that caused the most difficulty.

During the Christmas camping season, I visited the camps and saw the different approaches to planning they had. I noted down much that I felt needed to be dealt with in the year ahead. I found the first English-speaking camp I directed decidedly challenging. Four boys did not speak English and refused to understand my Spanish, and communication with the cook was difficult. But overall I felt it went well, and I believed a foundation had been laid for the future.

I looked forward to directing the inaugural camp to be held at our new Kimo jungle campsite. This was to be an English-speaking camp. We were to travel across the Andes by bus with an experienced driver from the Chanchamayo Bus Company. On 17 February 1977, we sent off at 7 am and by midday had reached Ticlio, 4800 metres above sea level. The campers were given a break here so they could have some fun in the snow. For quite a few this was a new experience. They were warned to move slowly because of the lack of oxygen at that height.

Our stop for lunch was at La Oryora (3600 metres). The final bus leg took us up very steep rises then down again, all on a frighteningly narrow road. The back of the bus seemed to hang over the edge as we rounded the corners. By the time we reached La Merced we were nearly at the campsite. We only had to cross the raging Chanchamayo River on the cable platform—with our luggage—and walk up to the campsite. I had told the girls before we set out that the bus trip was part of the camp, so I was pleased to notice new friendships had begun.

After such a long and tiring day of travel, I was glad we did not have to put up tents at this campsite. Instead we used the rickety old house on the property, which shook when people walked around or even turned over in their sleep. We slept in hammocks with mosquito nets to protect us from vampire bats upstairs. There was a lean-to kitchen downstairs, and to avoid having to collect water from the stream some distance away, we put out lots of containers every night to collect some of the abundant rain.

On our walks we discovered a crystal-clear pool for swimming under a waterfall. This was only a short distance from the house. It was a special feeling to have the waterfall cascading over your skin,

With Gladys and Victor Loyaza at Union Biblica, Lima.
1977

At Camp Kawai.
1977

and with the walk to the falls being so beautiful, this spot became one of my favourite places in Peru.

I was the only Australian at this camp. The girls came from Britain, the USA and European countries. Some were the children of diplomats and others of missionaries. One of the leaders, Nancy Black, was an experienced leader and helped me greatly. She was in Peru as a Wycliffe Bible translator to work on the Quechua language. I felt the camp was a happy, relaxed time, and I even got to prepare and enjoy some Australian foods.

Before camp I had arranged for the girls to go home with the leaders while I remained at Kimo until Mariano and the next group of campers arrived. When the girls left, I enjoyed the comparative quiet as I waited with the cook and other staff. The day passed and Mariano did not appear. Next day, at my request, I was taken into La Merced by one of our local helpers. I took the opportunity there to write home and have a cafe meal—a nice change from camp food. In the cafe I heard that the road to Tarma had been blocked by a landslide. I imagined Mariano's young people swapping buses with my campers so that he could continue to the camp and my campers could get home.

Returning to Chanchamayo, I waited expectantly, but Mariano's group still did not come. I heard later that there had been seventeen landslides on the road, and that our girl campers had taken twenty-six hours to get home instead of the expected eight. The two groups had met but had not been able to swap buses. Mariano accepted that he could not get through to me, so he found a church hall in Tarma and conducted a mini-camp from there, having Bible studies and visiting local sites before returning to Lima.

After a few days we heard that the road to Acombamba, where Nancy Black lived, was open, so those of us left at the campsite set out in a *colectivo*. The road was only open "after a fashion". Twice we had to get out and run through sections when our driver felt we would be less likely to be hit with falling rocks on foot than we would be in the car! This was another new Peruvian experience.

When we arrived in Acombamba, I called to see Nancy. She persuaded me to stay with her for a few days, so I arranged for the others to go back to Lima. I was so pleased to have the opportunity to learn more of her story and future work. When she was twenty-nine, she developed a rare type of cancer and was not expected to live. Now at forty-one she was in Peru learning Spanish and planning to go as a Wycliffe translator to an area where only Quechua was spoken. This, she told me, would involve her travelling to Junin, which was 4100 metres above sea level, then walking for at least eight hours up to 4500 metres, then down again to 3600 metres. There were no roads and it was impossible for aircraft to land, so walking was the only answer. This demanded a high level of fitness. Nancy's plan was to leave after Easter.

I appreciated these few days of rest and fellowship—I felt I needed them. I returned to Lima during the second week in March. Everything in my apartment was covered in Lima's notorious dust, and I swept up enough to start a small garden!

As I settled back to work at the Unión Bíblica office, I sensed a change was happening. Early in February I had overheard someone say of me, "It seems she doesn't need God. She is so efficient." I was devastated. I wrote that day:

> Oh God, how could it be? You know how much I want to live as you want me to. Without you I am absolutely useless. Help me please to be efficient in ministry without projecting what I am not. God, in myself I cannot change. I obstruct, obscure *your* light which ought to shine. I long to be your person here. Secure, so when words of uncertainty question my security, the inner peace will still be there. Help me please to *know* your intimate care.

Since then I had led my camps, but on returning I was warned some changes were likely to be made at the March meeting of the *junta directiva* (board). My work with camps had been under the direction of Petronio as Unión Bíblica General Secretary, but it had become evident to everyone that administration was not one of Petronio's strengths. At the board meeting the work was divided into five areas, with the person responsible reporting directly to the board:

1. Publication and promotion of the Spanish Unión Bíblica notes for the folk of Sierra—Petronio

2. Promotion of biblical materials in churches—Petronio

3. Finance and legal affairs—Victor Loyaza (voluntary)

4. Camps and schools—Lesley

5. Administration—Lesley

I found myself scared of the responsibilities I was being given, especially since I had been in the country for less than a year and was still learning the language, but I naively plunged on. I continued language lessons with Gloria and enlisted the help of a new friend, Viola, who was married to a Peruvian, in formulating a learning program. I knew discipline would be the key to my succeeding.

Other highlights of March 1977 included celebrating Mrs Clark senior's seventy-fifth birthday; having Berenice show her friendship by taking me to meet a teacher named Leonor Acosta, whom I hoped would be able to help me develop the schools' work; and experiencing the national obsession with football when matches between Peru and Ecuador, and then Peru and Chile were held in Lima. The whole city came to a standstill, with everyone shouting *"Arriba, Peru!"* (Come on, Peru!). My friends were all jealous because, through my involvement with hockey, I had once met the Peruvian soccer team. They were shocked to hear that I hadn't asked for autographs.

My final highlight, if it can be called that, was to spend some time as a patient in a Lima hospital. I woke up one day with diarrhoea but went to my language classes. On the way home I called in to see Gaye Mercier, an Australian nurse from Sydney, who, like me, was a CMS missionary. I slept for an hour at her place then went home. I began to feel worse, so I used a neighbour's phone to ring Gaye and ask her to come to be with me. During the night I became much sicker, and we telephoned Paul, who came in the morning and took me to the Clinica Anglo-Americana (British American Hospital). I was admitted and put on a drip, then, after investigations, discharged to Gaye's home. I stayed with her for a few days where I had time to reflect and write:

Thank you for the privilege of being here,
For the opportunity to see you working,
To experience your care.
To see my feebleness, yet strong in you.
To experience friendship
Not in words or meaningless phrases
But in giving—in a love which defies explanation,
A love that doesn't seek to take.

Thank you that you are refining, teaching me,
Gently, patiently but firmly.
It's exciting to see the way you are leading,
Each part fitting perfectly into plan.

Thank you that you are going to continue to make
My life a reflection of yours,
That with confidence I can know
My imperfections you will refine,
Gradually, thoroughly, lovingly,
In your time, in your way.

Thank you I can take courage
And wait for you.

FIFTEEN
Creativity and pressure

I listened to the radio as often as I could, hoping to speed up my language learning. There were many reports about the USA—Jimmy Carter had become president in January 1977. I heard virtually nothing about Australia until a train coming off the rails in Sydney was reported. It was quite a long time later that I found out the extent of the Granville train disaster and learned that a friend of mine, Tony Walker, was among the many who lost their lives. He left a wife and new baby.

Thefts, so prevalent in Lima, did not make the news, and despite my care I continued to be a victim of pickpockets. There was no government welfare in Peru and so much poverty, so in order to feed their families people resorted to stealing. I felt deeply hurt and angry when I lost precious gifts that friends in Australia had given me, even when I had hidden them in the bottom of my bag. One friend said she considered things she lost as her contribution to charity. I could not accept this, but at the same time I knew I had to learn, over and over again, not to cling to things, but only to God. Thieves regularly stole windscreen wipers, and people often took theirs with them when they locked their cars.

I was authorised to appoint a part-time secretary for myself, and also for Paul Clark to use as a typist when he needed to write a letter in English. I looked for someone who would continue to work when I was not watching her. She was to come to the office from 9 am to 1 pm each day. I interviewed several people, and our legal officer, Victor Loyaza, confirmed my choice of Ella Cueva. Ella proved a tremendous asset, and she and I became good friends.

I found my day's activities were varied. I spent the first hour or so writing necessary letters and fielding telephone calls. After that there were many meetings to attend and contacts to follow up. I became quite expert at travelling by *micro* and negotiating fares for taxis. I still found Lima's weather hard to cope with—it never rained, but the damp, coolish mist that hung over the city was like a dirty fog. I had a constantly runny nose.

Inflation continued to be rampant, and I noticed it particularly when I posted letters. The cost had risen over one hundred per cent in just a few months. I was fortunate as my salary came from Australia and the exchange rates were quite good. In this insecure climate, rumours spread quickly. I came home from a Camps Committee meeting one evening to find huge lines of cars waiting at the local gasoline station. They had heard that petrol prices were to rise the next day. Some waited for hours only to discover it wasn't true.

Queues formed everywhere, especially outside food shops. There was a shortage of the basics—rice, sugar and milk. There was no fresh milk at all; I soon became accustomed to the evaporated kind. As in so many cities in the world, most of the urban poor in Lima had left subsistence farming to seek a better life for their families in the city. Work was hard to find, and having sold all they possessed to pay for the trip to Lima, they found life extremely difficult. Many families were forced to live in *pueblos jóvenes*—large shanty towns on the outskirts of Lima—and watch as their children became slum dwellers. As I learnt more about these towns, I realised it was one of them that I had visited on my first Sunday in Peru.

The fifth of June was the anniversary of my arrival in Lima. I felt I had been there for a lifetime, yet there was so much I still did not understand about the culture. Everything took so long. It took me six hours, spread over two days, to open a bank account for the schools and camp work. With language classes as well as a busy work schedule, I felt exhausted. But I knew I must not take a break since I was responsible for planning and preparing for the next summer's camping season.

Finding experienced directors for the English-speaking camps was not difficult; missionaries were often keen to help. It was much harder to find directors for Spanish-speaking camps. In particular, very few were keen to go to our Kimo jungle site. As well as directors for each camp, dates, costs and other details had to be firmly set so that the prospectus could be printed by August. I also needed to find people to support the costs of poorer children so that scholarships for low-cost camps could be offered. We asked people to buy advertising space in our prospectus to help cover costs.

I seemed to spend much more time on the camps than the schools work because sudden urgent needs often overtook my long-term plans. With two others, I did manage to give a two-hour presentation on youth work at a pastors' and Christian workers' weekend retreat in late June.

Nine days before my birthday in July, I was taking a friend who was returning to England shopping when I stumbled and twisted my right ankle. I was still able to drive the car I had borrowed, so we decided to call in to see Gaye on our way home. She looked at my ankle, agreed it was probably a sprain and bound it up as a professional nurse would. During the night the ankle began to throb badly and was very painful. I phoned Gaye and she took me to the Clinica Anglo Americana, where an x-ray revealed a fracture of the fifth metatarsal bone. The treatment was a week completely off my foot to let the swelling go down and then five weeks in plaster.

Gaye invited me to stay with her for a while. I was still with her on my birthday. She suggested she would wash my hair that day—showering had been difficult with a plaster. Unbeknownst to me, she and Berenice had planned a surprise party that evening, and twenty friends turned up. It was wonderful. Once I went home, Leonor Acosta, my teacher friend, spent the first few nights with me. She wanted to make sure I could handle the stairs up to my apartment. I worked as much as I could from home. Once I felt able, my secretary Ella came each morning to take me to the office and bring me home about 1.30. The plaster finally came off on 13 August.

I had formed a good relationship with a number of American girls from the Union Church and had been leading them in a weekly Bible study on Friday nights. Many of this group would return to the States during the July school holidays, so numbers would be smaller. My broken ankle meant a short recess for this group.

Because I was keen to improve the training for camp leaders, one of my immediate tasks (with the support of the Camps Committee) was to organise a weekend training seminar for September. This involved a lot of work. In the midst of all this preparation, a much-needed replacement cable car for Kimo had to be organised. The original one was not designed to carry twenty or thirty campers across. We had a fundraising dinner in September, and I prepared a slide presentation with a script that I hoped someone else would read out. No one would do this, so in what I felt was my inadequate Spanish I did the job. Somehow people understood me.

During this period, I was conscious that I still had made little progress with the schools work. I knew quite a few teachers and asked their advice on how to move forward. Leonor was teaching at Colegio Maria Alvarado and invited me to start a Christian club to meet after school on Friday afternoons. I led Bible studies in Spanish for the first few weeks, then Leonor took over. Although the number of girls was small, I knew a larger number would attend the camps, so I felt the Friday group would be a great follow-up for girls who enjoyed and were blessed at camp.

I had a much-needed holiday in October 1977 and flew to Yarinacocha on the Ucayali River, where Nancy Black was now working. She had invited me to stay, and for the first three weeks I relaxed in a hammock all day and slept off the exhaustion of the past fifteen months. Leonor joined me for about ten days. This was a great time of seeing new things—for example, a huge python—and sharing fellowship with dear friends. I spoke only Spanish on this holiday and realised it had become my language because I began to dream in it.

When I returned to Lima, I was immediately flung into the final organising details for the twenty-six camps to be held from January to March 1978. It was a hectic time with a myriad of things to be completed. In mid-December we had a Christmas prayer breakfast to encourage support for the camps. Then I celebrated my second Christmas in Peru by visiting friends in response to their kind invitations. I ate so much at lunch that when I caught up with other friends in the evening I could only nibble at the food offered.

The Kawai camp had to be set up immediately after Christmas, and on New Year's Eve I was so exhausted that I slept through the noisy midnight celebrations.

SIXTEEN
Camps in quantity

The camping season, always such a busy time for me, got underway early in January 1978. My time was taken up fully with visits to all the camps. I both assisted and observed, and I dealt with many unexpected problems. When two campers were sent home for misbehaving, I had a time-consuming job dealing with the upset parents. I made a point of seeing off every group of campers as they left Lima, and I was always there to meet them on their return.

As well as administrating the overall program, I directed six camps. Ted Endacott from Scripture Union Victoria came to Peru to help us during this time. He brought some innovative ideas and was an instant hit with the English-speaking campers. The Kimo camps continued to offer very new experiences to the participants. Not only was Kimo the first time many had crossed the Andes or used toilets that were holes in the ground, they also saw and tasted, for the first time, avocados, papaya and mangos straight from the trees.

At my camps the studies were based on Ephesians, focusing on the character of God. Each day I went through these with the leaders, then they led their small groups with my modelling in mind. It all worked well. A number of the leaders were teachers who had graduated from three months of camping lectures I had given during 1977. Twenty-three came to a special teachers' camp planned as the culmination of the training. Here I had the opportunity to challenge them to think through their responsibility as Christian teachers in their schools. Samuel Escobar gave profound and moving Bible teaching, and the teachers left feeling refreshed and enthused for the start of the year.

I directed the final camp at the end of March. It was an evaluation camp where directors and leaders reported on their experiences and discussed both the positive things learnt and the things needing improvement. I was thankful when this group decided they needed more solid leadership training. They asked for this to begin in June, to prepare them for the next year's camps. I had wanted to do this, and now the idea came from the leaders themselves. I was thrilled.

Half way through the camping season, I was pleased to welcome Pauline Hoggarth to share my home for a few months. Pauline had been born in Peru where her parents were missionaries, had studied for a PhD in linguistics at Scottish and English universities, and was fluent in both Spanish and a dialect of Quechua. She was en route to Bolivia to work with Unión Bíblica there, stopping in Peru on the way to observe our work. I greatly enjoyed having her with me.

Just after I welcomed home one of our camps, I came to my flat and found the door had been forced open. My knees felt like water as I went through to find out what had been taken. The thief had gone through our wardrobes and every cupboard. Pauline and I felt violated. Both of our cassette players and alarm clocks were missing, as were many other special things. One hundred American dollars belonging to Pauline was gone. My greatest sadness was to lose the gold-plated Paper Mate pen my parents had given me when I left Australia. I treasured it so much that I never took it out of the house.

Pauline and I went to the police station. The policeman was apologetic but opened an empty drawer and said, with feigned frustration, "I'd love to take your statement, but I have no paper or pen." We headed outside and bought him both. He took our statements and we signed them. He then told us he held out little hope of finding the thieves. Unbeknownst to me, Pauline had a ring that the thieves had missed that she sold to buy us both new travelling clocks. I was deeply grateful for her generosity and thoughtfulness. This was another lesson teaching me that possessions were temporary and I must concentrate on what was eternal.

Meanwhile, I was trying to think of how to advance the schools work. I knew that if I was to work effectively in promoting Christian groups in Peruvian schools, I would have to know more about how their education system worked. My friend Berenice enabled me to get a job teaching at a lower middle-class national school two days a week. I was to teach Physical Education in the first and second grades and Religion in Grades 5 and 6. There were over forty pupils in each class and no text books. Many students had no pencil or book to write in.

With the challenges of trying to develop contacts and train teachers for the work in schools, as well as the demands of the camps work, I responded positively when Gaye Mercier suggested that we spend a few days down at Ica, a beach resort 303 kilometres south of Lima. Our CMS allowance enabled us to stay for a few days at the newly opened Holiday Inn there. We could not afford to eat at the Inn, but we enjoyed the luxury of the room. I loved sitting on the patio overlooking the small golf course, watching horse riders with the huge sand dunes towering above them.

I returned to prepare "realistic job descriptions" for the future needs of Unión Bíblica. I presented these at the April board meeting. I was due to go home to Australia on leave later in the year and the board had to work out who would ensure the work I had started was carried on. They found they needed several of the board members to take on additional responsibilities and to employ three new staff members in administration.

Over Easter I had another short break away. This time I went with Pauline Hoggarth and Ted Endacott to what is known as "the Switzerland of Peru". We took a bus to the lush green valley that runs between the Cordillera Negra (black range—no snow) and the Cordillera Blanca (white range—snow). This valley was the site of a large earthquake in 1962, when a town was wiped out after a portion of Huascaran, the highest and most impressive peak in Peru, broke off and sent earth, snow and mud crashing down, engulfing everything in its path. We enjoyed exploring the area, and, on a wet Easter Sunday, enjoyed a day inside our basic but comfortable accommodation at a Catholic Benedictine monastery.

May was Unión Bíblica Month and the focus in 1978 was on celebrating twenty-five years of Unión Bíblica camps. This involved having a celebratory dinner, a painting competition (coordinated by Mariano), a walkathon with over one hundred participants, an anniversary dinner and a thanksgiving service attended by over three hundred people. I was amazed and thrilled by the support all these functions received. During this time, I also preached at a number of our supporting churches.

Lesley departs for home leave.
Tribute by Mariano Lint.
1979

SEVENTEEN

First home leave

I was scheduled to leave Peru for home leave on 31 May 1979. Thanks to a generous gift from my friend from Townsville days, Kathy Connolly, I was able to return to Australia via the United Kingdom and Europe. I had been invited to speak in a number of places about the work of Unión Bíblica in Peru and I was keen to see more of Scripture Union's work. I was not expected back in Australia until mid-July.

The Camps Committee organised an exceptionally well-planned farewell dinner for me. During the second course, Mariano did a drawing while a group sang a song they had written about my time in Peru, simultaneously outlining what had been achieved and making fun of my ways of pronouncing Spanish words. After many nice things were said, I was presented with a beautiful leather handbag. I realised how much I was going to miss these people who had become so much part of my life.

I left by plane for London via Portugal. As I changed flights in Lisbon, I discovered my second suitcase was missing. Being fluent in Spanish by now, I understood their Portuguese reasonably well. After some time searching unsuccessfully, I was assured it would turn up later and they would send it to me in London. They asked where I would be staying, but having no idea, I gave them the address of the international Scripture Union office.

I was met in London by Scripture Union England's Nigel Silvester. Hearing my luggage story, he took me straight to the SU office to leave my bag and then shopping for some changes of clothes. I was expected that very afternoon at an SU camp leaders' training weekend! The UK prices confused me because the VAT was added to the tags on goods. I bought only absolute essentials as this was an unexpected expense. Nigel saw me off on a train to the camp. I was there just as an observer and found the experience lonely. I went for a walk one day and saw some beautiful flowers I didn't recognise: they were tulips. At the end of the weekend, I decided that our training course in Peru was superior to the one I had just attended.

On the Sunday evening I spoke at a Baptist church in the centre of London, and then John Prince and his wife, Moyra, visiting from SU Australia, drove me north to Scotland. We were attending an international Scripture Union conference at Carberry Tower Mansion House, near Edinburgh. When I met John Lane and Ron Buckland, more friends from SU Australia, I greeted them—as we did in Peru—with a hug. They were taken aback; Australians did not greet friends that way. But after that I had hugs whenever I saw them.

I was to translate from English into Spanish for international delegates. This was hard work. I wrote:

> This is such a beautiful place, Father. Fantastic to be with *so* many SU folk from around the world. The program is so full, Father, there is little time to *be* with *you*. Help me please to honour you as I do this translation work.
> It is so tiring.

At one point, when an African speaker used an excessive number of words to make his point, I waited before translating. Someone stood and complained that the translator was making a judgement about the material: "She is not translating every word!" I felt mortified, but the conference erupted into laughter.

I visited several other contacts in different parts of Scotland, speaking a number of times at churches about my work in Peru. John and Catherine MacPherson, whose home was the first I entered on arriving in Lima, had returned to Scotland for their children's education and I spent six lovely days with them. Even though I spoke at a number of meetings, I found this time relaxing and refreshing because I knew the family well. John was now the pastor at the Free Church at Dunkeld.

Returning to Greater London, I was billeted in Kent with a retired deaconess, Joan Marshall. I was to find out later that Joan and her sister, Betty, had lived next door to the Rev Don Douglass, my old rector from All Saints' Booval, when he was a boy, and that Betty had married Douglas Kahn, one of Don's closest friends. While I was staying with Joan, my lost suitcase finally turned up! I went to London and revelled in being just a tourist and visiting many of the wonderful historic sites. I also visited Betty and Douglas's home for an SU garden party—Douglas was the President of SU England.

The next leg of my trip was to Amsterdam in Holland. I visited those who had supported our work in Peru, saw Anne Frank's house, and then walked and walked until I saw scantily dressed women sitting in windows and realised I was in the red-light district. I hastily returned to my hotel. The next day I caught the train to Marienheide, Germany. I could not believe how close Holland and Germany were.

Scripture Union Germany's schools worker met me and took me home. As his family only spoke German and I only spoke English and Spanish, we had trouble communicating. He took me to see some of his work, after which I travelled to spend a couple of days with Claire, a French translator from the conference in Scotland, who entertained me royally and showed me some of Scripture Union's Swiss work.

The SU campsite in Lucerne was my next stop. The property overlooked Lake Geneva, and I feasted on cherries from the trees there. Language barriers made my stay difficult, so I was pleased to escape for a day into Geneva and see the famous Reformation Wall depicting some of the main figures of the Protestant Reformation. I also visited the church where John Calvin preached. Another Swiss SU worker, Armin Hoppler, who had shown great interest in our Kawai campsite, invited me to stay with him and his wife. I was surprised at the amount of Swiss chocolate waiting for me in my bedroom! Armin showed me further aspects of SU's work, and at the same time included a tour of Switzerland and a visit to the Principality of Lichtenstein. I was struck by how clean everything in Switzerland was.

I was due to return to England via Calais in France, so I caught the overnight train to Paris. I arrived early and was able to wander along the Seine, go to a service in Notre Dame Cathedral and walk up the Champs-Élysées (where I ate a strawberry crepe). I caught the train to Calais, the afternoon ferry to Dover and the train to London, where I spent the night at the home of Nigel Silvester's secretary. Next morning she took me by train to the airport for my flight home to

Sydney. Because of a breakdown we had to change trains half way there, and I feared we would miss the plane. We just made it—I was the last to board.

    I had a short thirty-first birthday as we crossed time zones on 18 July. I had to remember it alone. I changed into the nice outfit I had bought in London just before we reached Sydney. I was determined not to "look like a missionary" as my sister Debra had said I would.

EIGHTEEN
In Australia

I arrived in Sydney at 7.10 am on 19 July, cleared customs and caught the next flight to Brisbane. A large group of friends and family were waiting for me. I felt very tired, but at the same time surprised and thankful that so many had come to welcome me. This was a tangible reminder of the great prayer support my Australian friends and CMS had given me during the last three years. I knew that what I had achieved had been a result of the prayers of these people, and I decided to throw myself into reaching as many as possible during this holiday and deputation time.

Once home in Booval I met my niece, Kirsty, and baby nephew, Timothy, for the first time. That night I wrote: "Back in Australia for leave. What will this time be? Please guide me, Lord."

My first weeks were spent at home in Booval. I had to adjust to living again with my parents and four younger siblings. My mother and father just slotted me in as in the past, and, as then, I felt no warmth of welcome from my mother.

I spoke to many groups at All Saints Booval. All showed great interest in my life and work in Peru. My parents were at many of these meetings and others told me how very proud Mum and Dad were of me. I would have loved to have heard that from them. During this time I also enjoyed catching up with friends, talking, eating together and going on hikes. Special for me was having time with Toni, Gary, Kirsty and Timothy.

CMS and SU had arranged my deputation schedule. I spoke at a number of churches in Brisbane and then I was sent to visit North Queensland. I travelled up on *The Sunlander*, and when the train stopped at Mackay, I was surprised to find an old school friend, Mary, at the station to see me. She had read in the paper that I was coming north. She told me she had come to know Jesus as Lord and Saviour many years after I had first witnessed to her.

It was wonderful to catch up with friends in Townsville and to speak to different groups in Cairns. At one meeting there, people sat in a large circle outside. I wondered if my voice would cope. Praise God it did, but I was exhausted by the end. I was showing slides at another meeting and describing how far Peru was from Australia when someone asked, "Is it further away than Green Island?" (Green Island is twenty-eight kilometres north-east of Cairns.) I decided then that in future I would talk about how God answered prayer in my work rather than talk about Peru.

Back in Brisbane I was told that SU Australia was working to raise money to buy me a car in Peru. This was exciting news. I knew what a tremendous difference a car would make to my work and felt humbled that so many were prepared to be so generous. Both CMS and SU also invited me to Adelaide to speak. This gave me the opportunity to visit my sister Karen, her husband and daughters. Although not yet a believer, Karen had supported me in my work. Mum, Dad and I had continually prayed for her.

I was invited to speak at both the Queensland and Victorian CMS Summer Schools. Both of these were great opportunities to gain support for my work. I also spoke at the Victorian Beach Mission Thanksgiving evening. Before my turn, each beach mission team leader showed slides and talked about their mission. This time I had no slides to show and began to fear I wouldn't be able to hold the crowd's interest. Praise God, I did not need slides. God worked.

While I was in Victoria, I visited John and Janine Stewart, good friends of many years. After lunch John invited me to his study to talk. During this conversation I revealed how hopelessly inadequate I felt, even though others saw me as competent, and how this made me feel confused about who I really was. Although our discussion did not resolve any underlying issues, it did open a crack in my defences. It was the beginning of a process that would bring me inner healing and freedom from my past.

I had some time back in Booval with my family, and then, on 9 March 1980, a recommissioning service was held at All Saints. While I was anxious to be back in Peru, I felt reluctant to depart. I wrote in my diary: "Lord God, I have learnt so much during this time in Australia. Please go before me as I return to Peru."

Kimo.
1978

NINETEEN

Return to Peru

On 13 March 1980, my parents and some of my siblings farewelled me at Brisbane airport—this time without drama. My flight took me through Hawaii to Los Angeles. There I was met by Larry and Lois Dodds, Wycliffe translators from Peru, who were doing deputation work in Fresno, a city five-hour's drive north of LA. I went with the three Dodds children to Disneyland the next day and had a great time—their enthusiasm was infectious. They took me on a boat through the "Children of the World" exhibit, with the music of "It's a Small World After All" playing; "America Sings", an authentic paddle steamer trip; a bob-sled ride down the Matterhorn; the Thunder Mountain railway; and much more. I was transported back to the Disney television shows of the 1960s. Although Disneyland was not real life, I decided it was fantastic good fun.

My next stop was Mexico City, where I was met by Maurice and Iris Eastwick, SU workers who were trying to plant Unión Bíblica in Mexico. On the first day they took me to see the pyramids built by the Aztecs, and the following day to a basilica where an Indian was reputed to have seen the Virgin Mary and been given a painting. I was distressed to see people walking on bleeding knees for hundreds of metres, believing they would gain a hearing from the Virgin. As we travelled, we talked about our work and encouraged one another.

My next flight was direct to Peru. A famous actress was on board, but when we arrived at Lima, the crowd of more than twenty was there to meet me, not her!

At a "Welcome Home" lunch next day, I had a chance to hear how things had gone in my absence. I was then given a few days off to settle back. I discovered that the route of the Number 10 *micro* had changed—it now passed my building. My home was much noisier, and I certainly noticed the fumes that seemed to make their way easily up to my level. I noticed too that prices had sky-rocketed. I spent four times as much on cheese as I had before I left Peru. I was quickly reminded about the thieving in Lima when I heard that Paul's watch had been ripped off his wrist just the week before.

I was wondering what my role would be now since those who had taken over my work had simply carried on. I found myself mostly listening to folk as they spoke about their problems, and since I understood the issues, trying to sow the seeds of possible solutions. I did this as tactfully as I could so that they could come up with the ideas themselves and thus own them.

Just before Easter I went with a small group to Kawai. It was good to see how things were going there. I was disappointed not to see any signs of the huts for campers that should have been at least partly built by then, but I was told there had been delays and that things would start "soon". I was again struck by the grey sand of Peru, so different from the white Australian sand I had recently enjoyed.

On Easter Sunday, the English-speaking Unión Bíblica group organised a "sunrise service" for 7 am (though no one expected to see the sun—this was Lima!). I played my guitar and led the singing. When I got home, I wrote:

> A new creation! Christ is risen indeed!
> Cool wind caressing me,
> Dry grass prickling, thirsty open ground, calling for rain.
> Such is my life!
> I long to know a fresh saturating of your love
> That I might be whole again.
> Be done with the sin that wants its own way.
> I'm afraid, with the future unknown.
> I like the little world that I hold so firm.
> O help me let go,
> Learn humility and trust in your love today.

In April, I listened at a camps evaluation meeting to comments of appreciation about the leaders I had trained before I left. None of them, however, felt confident to take on a camp director role. I could see how much another leadership training course was needed and was thankful the Unión Bíblica directors agreed. I arranged to meet some of the other Camps Committee members at the Kimo campsite to confirm exactly where the main building, which was about to be built, should go. There was also a quick visit to Nancy Black en route. I was again overcome by the beauty and magnitude of the Andes—and by the unreliability of plans in Peru, when the others didn't arrive at the campsite when expected. I also discovered how unreliable hammocks are to sleep in: mine collapsed during the night. Fortunately, I wasn't hurt.

I felt I was gradually finding my place in the Unión Bíblica again.

Leadership training with Leonor.
1977

TWENTY

Major expansions

I discussed the schools work with Leonor, Berenice and Mariano, as well as two other volunteer camp leaders, Zoila and Maria. We agreed that another series of Bible studies for teachers could help challenge them to present the message of Jesus to their students. I was warned that Peruvians often say they will come to things and just don't turn up, but thirteen teachers came to our first session, and a nucleus made it to each study. As they talked, I began to realise it was much more difficult in Peru to establish any sort of club in a school than it was in Australia. Although I realised that the Australian model was unlikely to work, I presented it because I didn't know how else to proceed.

One evening a birthday party was held for one of the young teachers, and I was invited to join them. Birthday celebrations are very important in Peru. As the number of my young teacher friends grew, so the number of parties I was invited to grew. I found I was out late almost once a week. As well as this, I was involved three nights a week as an advisor in youth work, either through my church or the schools work. Many people enjoyed coming to my apartment, and I always felt obliged to feed them. It all became too much, so I suggested I meet them once a month at church and only occasionally at my home.

One talented young lady had a very difficult family situation and attached herself to me. She chose my home as her place of retreat. I would come back from the office or even late at night, exhausted, and find Jackie (as we called her) waiting to talk. She was one of the few upper-middle-class people in the group, and through her I met yet another group of fun-loving young people. They would often be at my apartment, even at 9.30 or 10 at night, waiting for me to join them at the pizzeria. They wouldn't take no for an answer. I became more and more tired.

By this time I had become aware of problems in my relationships at Unión Bíblica. I felt these were due to misunderstandings, but I was devastated to find that I had unintentionally hurt some people and that their hurt had grown into real resentment. I found their criticisms hard to take. After one sleepless night, I read 2 Corinthians 7:10: "For godly grief produces a repentance that leads to salvation and brings no regret, but worldly grief produces death." This helped me realise that good could come from criticism, and I prayed: "Thank you for assuring me of this. Help me to get back on an even keel. O my God, help me. Help me love, not hurt others unintentionally. Show me when I am about to get it wrong. Help me see and stop."

In June 1980 I came down with a virus and was in bed for four days with a high temperature. A strike by rubbish collectors, along with Lima's damp winter air, made being sick an unpleasant experience. I made a point of visiting Berenice on her birthday. A Camps Committee retreat in Kawai the same month was a moderately positive time, but I felt we needed new blood if the work was to go ahead and not just be maintained. I knew I needed time to draw apart, pray and consider what God was saying about the way forward, so I planned a couple of days away in July.

I seemed to have one problem after another when preparing for a leadership training camp for secondary students. Finally it happened, with thirty-nine campers and seven leaders. I took studies on the seven churches in Revelation and felt the camp was a significant milestone in the lives of many present. Both teachers and students went back to school keen to encourage the members of their Unión Bíblica groups to pass on the message of God's love. I knew it was not easy to have groups in schools that had morning, afternoon and evening lessons, with few breaks in between. But I was reminded of the saying *Caminante, no hay camino, se hace camino al andar* (Traveller, there is no road, the path is made by walking). I prayed God would guide me as I walked.

Jackie was leaving to study in the United States, so I took her with me for my short break. We went to a monks' retreat at Huaraz, north of Lima. She had been a great asset on a number of camp teams, and I knew I was going to miss her dropping in. Mariano arranged for me to speak about our schools work to students in their final years in a couple of schools. I was very nervous speaking to such a large crowd, but with God's help I managed.

In September our second leadership training course began. Forty-six enrolled, a number of them sponsored by their churches. I wrote:

> Much potential for the Lord to do great things—but still I feel "mixed up". I long to be at peace, to walk each day in a disciplined, orderly way, really loving others with heart, mind, soul and strength, long to be "leaping like a calf released from the stall" (Malachi 4). How super heaven will be—but *life* begins here and now, and I lack the peace I crave.

As the course progressed, I became even more aware of how much I still did not understand Peruvian culture. I seemed to make so many mistakes and felt devastated when something I did hurt someone. One person told me that I came across as hard, aggressive and proud. I prayed again and again to be made soft and sensitive. I felt certain God had sent me to Peru, and I longed for others to come to know Jesus.

The climax of the course was a camp in December 1980 at Kimo. There was a sense of oneness on the day-long trip across the Andes. The experience of being in the jungle, studying the Bible (alone and together), singing, walking to the waterfall and picking fruit from the trees made this a very special time. It was the highlight of the course. A few days after returning, elegant certificates were presented. I knew how proud the students were, and that many certificates would be framed and hung on walls.

Gaye Mercier had gone back to Australia on home leave and had given me permission to use her car while she was away. It was such a help while I was eagerly awaiting news of the car that Scripture Union Australia was raising money for. Although the funds arrived in May, it was not until the end of October that I was able to pick up my beige, window-tinted Datsun Estanza sedan. The official said, "Make sure you fill up with petrol." About fifty metres down the road, before a petrol station was even in sight, the car stopped, empty. I was thankful that Berenice had come with me, so she remained in the car while

I walked back and demanded fuel to get us to a petrol station. They came up with just enough.

My first job on the car was to have a second alarm fitted. Car thefts were so frequent in Lima. The dust-filled atmosphere meant that the vehicle needed daily cleaning, so I employed a man to do this. But I noticed that if I left any loose change in the car, it disappeared. Then, when I had my first flat tyre, I found my jack was missing. Ultimately, I had to dismiss my car cleaner.

Having the car enabled me to drive a number of the young people home after I had been out with them. Great as this was, I found it resulted in even more, much later bed times.

I directed one of the early January 1981 camps, held at Kawai, with a group of inexperienced leaders. Our campers were eleven- to thirteen-year-old boys. On the last day I was told that Yolanda, a mother of five children who had been an assistant cook for our camps several times, had died in Lima after surgery. (Paul later found out that, because she was poor, her organs were used for those who could pay.) I sat with the grieving family when the body finally arrived home for burial. I was numbed by Yolanda's death. I knew her well and she had named one of her children Lesley after me. I remained behind for the funeral and was able to drive the family to the Roman Catholic church, then to the cemetery.

On the way to Kimo for another camp, our bus full of campers was stopped and told that no one could pass unless each person had a yellow fever injection. I had papers showing I had been vaccinated, but many on the bus had to be given the jab then and there. I protested strongly when I saw the same needle was to be used for more than one person. I hastily bought sufficient needles for each person on my bus to have a clean one. I was afraid my supply would be used again for others later, but at least I kept our group safe.

I took a few days off after the last camp and went to Acombamba to stay with Nancy. I needed time to be quiet with the Lord. I wrote my prayers and thoughts down each day, as was my habit. Many times I thanked God for so much—his grace, his love, his calling, his gifts, and especially for the beauty of the world he had created and given us to enjoy. Yet as in the past I also cried out to God to change me:

> What good is fear? … Help me to learn to relax in
> the presence of others and learn to listen to them.
> Unintentionally I alienate others. Help me not to …
> You, Lord, are my shepherd. What do I lack? Nothing!
> Help me believe it.

While I used to sing God's praises, I felt that my life was singing out the opposite. I asked myself:

> Do I manipulate others? I don't want to do that. I want
> people to know your Calvary love, to be drawn close to
> *you*. You know me through and through, the guilt within,
> the sin. My God, make me conscious of your grace,
> do a work of re-creation.

I told God time and time again that I needed help with patience, love and self-control: "I don't know how to administer all you have given me … I don't want to come on too strong in relation to others."

After that much-needed break with Nancy, I came back to Lima to the busy after-camps activities and the need to develop the schools work. I was concerned to find that there were days when I didn't want to leave the house. On one such day I wrote: "I will go because there is that meeting at Maria Alvarado school. I feel so far away from God … I read the Bible yet do not learn." I couldn't work out why I was feeling that way.

I still had visitors to my house regularly. At a lunch I gave for the eight members of the Inter-Schools Committee, I was told by Paul Clark that Leonor was going to Chile to work with Unión Bíblica there. She was one of the most positive, insightful members of the committee and a good friend from whom I often sought guidance. I knew I would miss her greatly. The day after this meeting, I had thirty of the camp leaders over for lunch. It was worth the effort, even though tiring for me, because I could see that Unión Bíblica was growing.

In spite of my busyness, I did have some times of relaxation. I continued to enjoy playing hockey, and I was still a member of the Lima Cricket and Football Club. I also went there to play squash and swim.

Unexpected things often interrupted my work plans. For instance, our caretaker at Kimo, Manuel, was arrested on the way to Lima and imprisoned. I immediately went to the police station. The police thought I was a nun (I did not tell them otherwise) so I was allowed in to see him. The crime of which he was accused had been committed in Arequipa, a town about 750 kilometres south of Lima. Unión Bíblica agreed to pay any costs needed to prove his innocence. I went with him to Arequipa to face the charges, accompanied by a policeman. When we arrived, we were told that a man of the same name had already served a sentence for the crime. It was a case of mistaken identity, and of being considered guilty until proven innocent. Manuel received no apology or recompense for this trauma. Without Unión Bíblica's financial help, he would have languished in prison for many months.

Back in Lima, I began the organising of the next camps' leadership training course. I also attended a cross-cultural communications course in Bolivia, staying with Pauline Hoggarth. The two-week intensive course was challenging and helped me to review my time in Peru. I wrote:

> I've been an agent of change in Unión Bíblica in Peru, yet I am coming to a watershed. I've seen many areas where the changes have been good—the camps work has grown, the leadership courses have been effective, an embryonic schools work established—but unless I come to grips with who I am, learn to walk beside, together with others, I have nothing more to offer. Please, Father, by the end of this course give me the tools I need to begin anew, and the courage to do it.

I wanted what I learnt not to be just head knowledge but head-and-heart knowledge, working out in my whole life. In spite of my praying and my desire to work effectively with others, I still had great unease about what the people I worked with thought of me.

After the course, Pauline and I had a few days' holiday together. I talked some things over with her. In my diary I wrote out three personal goals: (1) Work out how to have a consistent, realistic, meaningful time with God; (2) Work out how to affirm those I work with in a positive way; (3) Seek God's forgiveness every time I see someone as a threat.

I returned to Lima to a busy time of meetings, planning and speaking engagements. At the Camps Committee meeting I was told that they did not want new people to join them. I wondered how we were going to grow the work if we weren't open to people with fresh ideas.

The work in schools, however, *was* growing, and, with the help of Emperatriz, Elsa and Marisol (the three teachers the Camps Committee would not welcome), I put forward a new initiative: *La Busqueda Vocational* (Find your vocation) to help young people make careful and godly decisions about their careers. We aimed to have sessions at as many schools as possible. I spent long hours on the phone, getting people from different career areas to come to speak and answer questions.

I also had quite a few speaking engagements. At the Pentecostal church at Vivarte, I was quite taken aback when I was asked to "open" their new toilet. It was a hole in the ground with a toilet seat over it, surrounded by hessian. I was to say a prayer and then use it. I was thankful the hessian was thick!

Leadership seminar.
1976

TWENTY-ONE

Bombshell

On 19 November 1981, I was having lunch at Gaye's place with other Aussie CMSers in Lima when I received a phone call. I was asked to come immediately to a meeting with three members of the board. I had no idea what it could be about. Without warning, they gave me the devastating news that I was to leave Peru. They told me I had emotional problems and needed to return to Australia for help. I was to leave in a week.

I left the meeting utterly dejected. How could this happen? I felt certain Peru was where God wanted me. How could I face my people at home as such a failure? Deep inside, though, I knew the board members were right—all my relational difficulties showed that. I was to get help at home. Perhaps it was now or never for me to live happily.

Gaye was at my apartment waiting for me. I realised then that she had been involved in the decision. I was in a daze. It was all too much. Gaye took control, and over the next nine days helped me sort and pack. At night, when I was alone, I cried out to God for understanding: "How am I going to go through with this? It's real, final. I just can't go it alone. My God, where are you?"

My *Daily Light* reading next morning, which I read after an almost sleepless night, included Isaiah 42:3: "A bruised reed he will not break, and a dimly burning wick he will not quench." There were so many things I could not understand. The training course was going so well; the schools work seemed to be expanding; the car, provided for me so generously, had only been used for a year. Leaving didn't make sense. I asked myself how I had got into this mess.

I felt particularly concerned for my parents—not only that I had to face them as such a failure but also that they would have to face being the parents of a failure. I prayed: "My God, at the moment I can't see any good coming out of this … O my Father, please provide for me people who will really love and care for me—and Father, provide for my parents too."

I had occasional moments of peace and acceptance of the situation. I thought of the verse "Though the fig tree does not blossom, nor fruit be on the vines, the produce of the olive fail and the fields yield no food, the flock be cut off from the fold … yet will I rejoice in the Lord" (Habakkuk 3:17–18). I clung to "GOD, the Lord, is my strength" and prayed, "Please make it so." I knew I couldn't change the situation and was getting to the point where I just wanted to get it over and done with.

Clearing out my apartment was a lot of work. I found it hard to decide what to take and what to give away or throw out. Sorting papers was the worst. As I worked, I oscillated between acceptance and non-acceptance. I received a note from Nancy in Chile, saying, "My love and prayers go with you. Just remember there is light at the end of the tunnel." I accepted this, but could not believe it.

Berenice, Mariano and a number of other friends called asking why I was leaving. I told them I was being sent home to rest. I didn't think they understood why, and I must say, neither did I. The reason I had been given sounded so trite. My nightmare continued. A couple of days before I was to fly out, I spent time with Samuel and Lily Escobar. Samuel said, "Even though you have many exceptional gifts, you don't accept yourself." I knew it was the truth.

On the day of my departure, I was driven to the airport where seventy or eighty people were gathered to say goodbye. They could not believe I was leaving. It was a good, positive farewell, but I felt numb and unable to respond adequately. I simply waved and walked through to the plane.

TWENTY-TWO

Wilderness of misery

On the plane the numbness gradually wore off, but I felt totally desolate. I was overwhelmed by a sense of failure. I had failed my family, my church, CMS, Unión Bíblica, my friends. Those who were sending me home seemed to have put all the focus on my mistakes and taken no account of what I had achieved. I thought of the lives I had touched through camps and schools work—so many had come to the Lord and grown in their walk with him. I felt deeply hurt, and afraid. I prayed I would not let bitterness take root.

I read the letter I had been given to take to CMS and was shattered. I felt betrayed by those I had trusted. The reasons I was being sent home were things I had not been told, and I felt sure I could have handled hearing them and put things right. I plunged further into despair.

I barely coped as I left the plane in Los Angeles. Somehow I managed to get through customs without crying, then found that a couple, Norman and Susie Hoffman, friends of someone I knew in Peru, had come to meet me. Susie gave me a hug and I burst into tears. They didn't ask questions, just drove me home, gave me something to eat and drink, and put me to bed. Susie sat with me till I slept. The next day they took me back to the airport for my flight to Sydney via Honolulu.

I felt God had abandoned me.

It took me some time to find my bags and go through customs in Sydney. I wondered who would be there to meet me and what they would say. No one was waiting. I phoned Marie Dawson, the wife of CMS Overseas Secretary Peter Dawson, who told me that Peter and Beryl Box, another CMS couple, had been there, but left. They soon returned and welcomed me, but thankfully didn't ply me with questions.

Peter and Beryl drove me to Chatswood to stay with Beth Watley, secretary to the CMS Australia director. I shunned company and hid in my room when Beth had visitors. I couldn't face church on Sunday. I thought about Peter's massive failure at Jesus' trial and asked God to please use me in the future as he did Peter. I wrote: "What do you require of me? To be just in every situation, to love kindness and to walk humbly with you. Please help me do this. Teach me humility."

At night I found myself dreaming of Kawai and other special places in Peru. I would wake feeling desperately sad about the way I had left. I remembered so many precious young people whom I knew God had blessed. I managed to write a positive letter to my supporters, but I was not at all sure it was real.

It took me two weeks to open and read the letters given to me on my departure. I was amazed to find how much Berenice wanted my support, how Lucy relied on my comments, how Marisol looked to me for encouragement. Many more expressed distress that I had left. When I spoke to Jackie in the United States, she said that our friend Juan Carlos had written to her, saying, "They don't know what a jewel they are throwing away." As encouraging as these letters were, I knew that my friends had not seen the "me" that was lonely, not coping, overreacting and responding inappropriately when threatened.

CMS had arranged for me to have counselling with Michael Corbett-Jones at the Anglican Counselling Centre. I felt scared but hopeful as I went to my first session. Since it was late in December, Michael used this time to give me some basic strategies to use when I went home to my family in Booval for Christmas.

I flew to Brisbane on 24 December. I knew this was not going to be an easy time for either me or my parents. I hardly remember that Christmas. I was encouraged to hear about Ian's strong, growing Christian faith, but I continued to find it hard to relate to Mum. She didn't know what to say to me and I didn't know what to say to her. I avoided going to the Queensland CMS Summer School. I couldn't face those who had supported me so lovingly.

I didn't know whether I was going back to Peru or not. Then on 9 January I received a letter telling me that my drums were packed and ready to be sent to Australia. I found this so confusing. Was this really the end of Peru for me? I was not ready to face that. I kept remembering wonderful times at the camps, especially one camp at Kimo when so many seemed to be deeply blessed through the studies from 1 Timothy. It was straight after this camp that Gaye had said, "When are you going to deal with your personal problems?"

My time at home was really hard, and I was thankful when 19 January 1982 came and I could fly back to Sydney to continue my counselling with Michael.

Kawai.
1980

TWENTY-THREE

Towards healing

My first appointment for the year with Michael was two days after I returned to Sydney. He suggested I lie on a mattress on the floor while he sat beside me. He then encouraged me to breathe deeply, explaining that I had controlled my feelings by my breathing and that breathing deeply would put me in touch with them. He said he felt I had buried my emotions deep as a defence mechanism. Releasing these feelings would happen gradually if I worked on my breathing, and eventually I would resolve whatever was holding me back. He told me I would see the light at the end. At that moment, I was very doubtful.

At my next session, a week later, Michael again assured me that as I lay on the floor and breathed deeply, I would find release. Feelings of loss began to surface, but I couldn't cry. I was still blocking so much. A few days later I wrote: "Lord God, I want to be a wholly integrated person. I believe *you* have the best in store for me. I long to know the meaning of the promise 'If the Son sets you free, you will be free indeed.' "

By the end of February, Michael had helped me accept that some devastating trauma had happened in my life, probably before I had turned three, and that this small child within me was calling out for help. My confidence in Michael was growing and I trusted him, but I didn't understand what this trauma was about. I wrote:

> Please help me feel the needy, helpless child in me.
> I can't see it yet but I hope one day freedom will come.
> Thank you that you promise that nothing will be beyond what I can bear with your help ... I feel fragile. I want love, to be held ... there is so much I don't understand ... keep me within your plan ... Remove my barriers, defences, Lord God.

I kept praying that I would continue to read the Bible and pray for others. One day I was wondering what I had done in the light of eternity, so I listed over thirty individual names of people who had come to the Lord through my work and become truly committed Christians. I began to write down the names of the leaders and school groups who had enthusiastically taken part in my training classes and camps. I knew God *had* worked through me. I suddenly stopped my writing; it wasn't helping. It was no good going over old ground. I had to move on, resolve the issues and truly be able both to love people and let the warmth of their love and affection reach into my inmost self.

On Good Friday I went for a bushwalk and cried out to God to show me the power of his resurrection. I felt I was making no progress in the counselling. The session after this was bitterly disappointing. I decided to catch the hydrofoil to Manly to try to find some peace. I walked along the beach and caught the last ferry back, then walked the streets of Chatswood until 3 am. I was at the point of not caring if I lived or died.

At the next session with Michael, I focused on a time when I was twelve. One night I was studying, feeling cut off from the rest of the family watching TV. Michael suggested I go and tell my parents what I was feeling at the time. I couldn't do it; I had to be seen as coping. Then I had an unexpected insight from an even earlier time. I expressed it by saying, "I need you, Mummy and Daddy, to love me, to want me, to appreciate me—to hold me and hug me—just because I am me. But if you're not going to, if I can't be special just by being me, then I'm going to make myself special, and then you will appreciate and notice me." I realised that I had had this was a feeling for a long time but had not acknowledged it.

I started to read books on the needs of children. I learnt that a child needs love most when least loveable; that children are not basically mean, vengeful or hostile unless they have been made fearful and insecure; that many studies had found what happens in the first two years is of paramount importance; that it is instinctive for children to want to please their parents; and that it can be devastating if children receive criticism instead of love. I also learnt that what passes as laudable ambition is often simply an effort to compensate for feelings of inferiority—it is saying, "Love me or, if I am not worthy of that, at least notice me." I felt I might be beginning to understand my problems.

Michael suggested I should go to Melbourne for two weeks of intensive daily sessions with a psychiatrist. I agreed—I would do anything to get better. I was to stay with an ex-CMS missionary who had worked in Iran some years before and her sister. They welcomed me and gave me the space I needed.

At my first appointment, the psychiatrist helped me craft a statement of what I was looking for: "I, Lesley, make a definite commitment that, to the best of my ability, I will be honest with my feelings and endeavour to express them in an appropriate way. I will not try to 'defend' God." As I started the therapy, I cried out to God for help, telling him how worthless I felt and how afraid I was: "Where are you, God? Why won't you hear me? Respond? Help me, please." Each day, as another layer was peeled back, all I felt was despair.

I still felt a strong pull to go back to Peru, but I knew it was to see my friends, not to return to the work. I could not face the schools work again. The prospect of staying in Australia also scared me. On the weekend between my weeks of counselling, my friend Barbara and I went rowing on the Yarra River and unexpectedly met Ted Endacott, who had helped me a few years before in Peru. We had coffee together, but I didn't want to talk about the work in Peru or why I was home.

When I returned to Sydney, I wondered if anything had been achieved through this Melbourne trip. I certainly had cried often, but I still lacked any sense of peace. Deep within I had a yearning to feel satisfied and secure. I began to doubt God's promises, and I reminded him of all the prayers I felt he had not answered. I asked, "Why?"

> What am I doing or not doing that is hindering your work in me? It is five months since I left Peru, and what have I achieved? All I feel now is hopelessness and despair … Somehow touch me so that I know you care.

With Lily and Samuel Escobar. 1986

TWENTY-FOUR

Refocussing

I was still receiving loving letters from friends in Peru telling me of my effective work there, but they made me feel even more alone and hopeless. I wondered if I would ever again feel it was good to be alive. I could see no light anywhere. I had loved to entertain in Peru, and when the curate and his wife in the Sydney parish where I was living invited me to dinner, I had a delightful evening. The meal and the company were superb. I told God I would so enjoy the opportunity to entertain like that again.

CMS were paying me a home-leave allowance, but eventually they let me know that this would soon stop. I needed to find a job to support myself. I applied for a couple of teaching positions, but as I could only work four days a week (I needed Thursdays off for counselling), I was unsuccessful. I also found my years in Peru were not a help. I failed to even get an interview in several jobs I applied for. I prayed that I would remember what I had learnt about worldly values in Peru and not get absorbed in Australian values again.

Finally I saw an advertisement from an educational supply company, applied and got the job. I was excited at the prospect of working again. I promised God I would give twenty percent of what I earned to his work. I wanted to show in this job that I had learnt from my time with Michael and could relate to people in a relaxed, less stressed way. I knew I needed a car for the job and my young brother, Ian, gave me $2000—I was overwhelmed with thankfulness for him. CMS told me of a car dealership in Moss Vale that found good cars for missionaries and I bought a 1976 Subaru wagon. I felt ready to start work.

I was told that my zone was to be west of the Pacific Highway and north of the Parramatta River, as far as Katoomba. I had to contact schools, make appointments to show them the books, take orders and deliver these to the office. They would then send the books to the schools. I was to be paid according to the sales I made.

On my first day, I went to the office and loaded up my car with books. I managed to make several appointments, asking to have time with both the junior school and senior school librarians and, if possible, subject teachers as well. On my first visit, I sold one book. I discovered that selling for commission was hard work—my first pay from L&S Educational Supplies was just $36. I used to pray as I went to the schools that the Holy Spirit would help me show Jesus to those I met. Often I made only one or two dollars after all the work I had done. One day, after weeks of work, I sold $700 worth of books and made nearly $100.

Needing more money, I tried to augment my income by letterbox dropping. I received $36 for ten hours of walking up and down hills, trying to reach inaccessible letterboxes. It was not worth the effort.

I was thankful, though, that I could make my own appointments because I could keep Thursdays free to see Michael. At one appointment I felt I had a small breakthrough. At each counselling session, feelings had been surfacing—I wondered when, if ever, I would understand what my real issues were. At the end of June I started to grieve my lost, gone-forever childhood. I realised I had, as long as I could remember, felt like a replacement child, conceived three months after the twins died at birth. I didn't know what my parents had said that made me get this message. Now, with the help of counselling, I had started to think this could not be true. No, I had been conceived in their love for each other, in the midst of their grief. I had carried a false feeling for years. I wanted to get to know this untrue feeling so that I could let it go forever. Suddenly I began to feel it was possible that I might be accepted.

Michael warned me there was more to come, and left me alone in the room to come to terms with what I had experienced. Later we walked together to the station. This became a pattern for the rest of the year. He explained that he wanted to make sure I was all right.

I was beginning to feel I had overstayed my welcome where I was living, so when I was told that the sister of CMS Federal Secretary Alan Cole had a small flat attached to his home in Turramurra that I could use for four months, I moved there. I was glad of the space to sort out the books I kept in my car. I couldn't help worrying about where I would go next. I asked God to help me cope with not belonging anywhere. I still couldn't hear him. I was often on the point of tears, but couldn't cry.

One Friday, when my work took me to the Blue Mountains, I decided to rent a room at Echo Point so that I could go bushwalking on the Saturday. I knew I would find it good to be in nature again. I walked down the Giant Stairway. Alone in the bush, with no one to hear, I shouted out my feelings. Michael had suggested that my sense of never being good enough had begun with the birth of my sister, Karen, and had increased with the birth of each subsequent sibling. This, and the fact that my mother's continual refrain was that I could do better, meant that my feelings of inadequacy became deeply embedded. I had tried so hard to be good enough but never succeeded, attempting to do the work of two because I thought I was a replacement for twins. I didn't understand why Mum could never say, "Well done!"

Caloundra.
1983

TWENTY-FIVE

More perplexity

At the end of August 1982 I received a letter from Ted in Melbourne suggesting we explore whether there was more to our relationship than friendship. This made me note down what I felt were essential attributes in a marriage partner. I wanted someone I could truly love and serve and who would truly love and look after me. We would share honestly with one another in every way. He would have a quiet, gentle confidence and not need to prove himself. Together our walk with God would grow and deepen.

I found the month of October very difficult. That was the last full month I had been in Peru. I didn't want to go out and face people. I also had to make the decision to resign from CMS. I had begun to see that returning to Peru could not be an option.

I flew with a friend, Lyn Perini, to Melbourne and stayed with Barbara. I visited Ted and we talked for hours. We had been corresponding weekly, and we agreed that he would come to Queensland with me to spend Christmas with my family. At my December counselling session, I had another breakthrough: I knew God loved me. I felt I had never really known that before. I also began to understand Mum more. She had lost her own mother when she was very young and her father had abandoned her in her teen years. She had no one to turn to. My father became her security and provider, but after the twins died and I came along, she could never be the mother I needed. As a result of this, from an early age God drew me to himself.

Ted flew to Sydney on 23 December. We packed my car up and set out for Ipswich. Jim and Carole Holbeck were in Armidale, so we stayed overnight with them and had a noisy rattle in the car fixed. We stopped at Cunningham's Gap—and Ted told me he could see no future in our relationship. I was stunned. I couldn't understand why he had come. He must have been unsure before coming and the trip had confirmed it. We arrived in Booval on Christmas Eve, and I explained to my family that we were just friends.

I journaled that night about how much I was hurting. I had thought he was the one for me. I prayed, "Help me to trust you. Will there ever be a husband I can give myself to?" Ted stayed until 28 December. It was a strange time, but at least I was grateful we had clarity.

New Year's Day 1983 made me wonder what the year would bring. I thought again about my feelings of being a replacement, and I asked God: "Why did the twins die? My life would have been *so* different if they had lived. Mum would not have had the profound grief that she passed on to me. Lord God, will you give me someone who will truly care for me, husband me?" I knew this was what I wanted, but even more I wanted to know God's peace and, from that peace, be able to reach out to others.

On 2 January Ian told us that he and Glenda, his lovely girlfriend, were engaged. I was so glad he had found such a perfect partner.

Staying with my family underlined that I still had issues needing to be resolved. I often found I would be by myself sewing or doing some job while all the others were in the kitchen talking. I couldn't reverse the pattern of years. I was afraid to get close to anyone or let anyone get close to me, fearful of being hurt again.

I did go to the Queensland CMS Summer School that year. People didn't ask me too many difficult questions. I was especially pleased to catch up with John and Gayelene Harrower, who spoke about their work in Buenos Aires. After Summer School I had a short holiday on my own on the Sunshine Coast. I spent this time pouring out my heart to God, sometimes in English and sometimes in Spanish. I asked God to help me find contentment and happiness as a single person.

After this break I headed back to Sydney to continue selling school resources. I moved to Artarmon with Truda Gaunt, who attended St Paul's Chatswood, and arranged to return to Michael for counselling, which meant keeping Mondays free for appointments.

Despite the fact my area had been expanded, I barely made enough to live on at L&S Educational Resources. I started to go door-to-door in the Artarmon area, selling Avon. The small amount I earned from this took a long time to come to me. I couldn't do anything more, so

I cried out to God to provide for me—I had almost started to feel he had given up caring. Things got particularly desperate when one Wednesday I sold only $10 worth of books, and nothing at all on Thursday or Friday.

That Friday night I received two letters. One was from CMS in response to my letter of resignation, with a sizeable lump sum resettlement payment included. The other letter said, "This gift is for yourself. We love you and care for you. The Lord has placed on our hearts to send you this cheque. It is a gift from the Lord with completely no strings attached. Please receive it wholeheartedly with no sense of obligation, for 'He gives freely to those he loves.' With all our love, Your friends." Inside was a cheque for $500.

In June 1983 I moved in with Don and Margaret Douglass in Chatswood. They knew me from Booval days and accepted me utterly. I became part of their family activities and would remain with them until I went home for Christmas and Ian's wedding. In July I was offered and accepted a job at St Paul's School, a new Christian school in Cranbrook, near Penrith. It was for half a day a week teaching PE. I felt very rusty, but I wondered if this was the beginning of reclaiming my teaching career. I added the half-day's teaching salary to my book-selling and Avon takings. It was a help.

Before returning to Sydney I had flown to Melbourne for further sessions with the psychiatrist, and now my weekly counselling sessions with Michael were enabling me to work through more layers of "no good" feelings. This often left me in emotional turmoil. My desire to be married constantly surfaced in my thinking, and I had to keep praying, "Father, I am prepared to go through life alone, though I don't want to. What I want more than anything is for others to know you through me."

In August I visited John Waterhouse at Albatross Books and suggested I sell suitable Christian books to the schools I visited. I arranged to carry samples he selected and return, hopefully, with orders for him. I was to be paid twenty percent commission. I felt pleased that at least I would be trying to get Christian books into schools.

Ridley College bookshop.
1984

TWENTY-SIX

Moving south

In October 1983 the phone rang, as it often did, in the Douglass house. Don called me, saying a John Wilson from Melbourne wanted to speak to me. I knew two Melbourne John Wilsons. One was the psychiatrist I had seen there, the other was the Old Testament lecturer at Ridley College.

It was the latter, and Don was pleased to hear that John had rung to offer me a job starting in 1984. I was to be the first full-time manager of the Ridley College Bookshop in Melbourne. I was thrilled and immediately accepted the offer. I thought how amazingly God had prepared me for this position: I had worked as a teenager in the university library; I had administrative, educational and organisational experience; and recently I had learnt something about the marketing of books and audio visuals in the secular field.

I had my last counselling session with Michael in December. I thanked him for being such a skilled and committed counsellor and helping me find God's love in a new and penetrating way. He said it had been a privilege to work with me for the past two years.

I headed home to Booval in time for Debra's twenty-second birthday on 16 December. The day after I arrived, Mum gave me a vest she had made out of red wool from an old jumper I had loved. I spontaneously gave her a decent hug. I was amazed at the difference in our relationship, and thanked God. Sadly, on Christmas Day, she turned very negative. I prayed, "Please, Lord, help her discover your love in a new way."

Ian and Glenda were married on 2 January 1984. By that stage I had talked a lot to my mother. My adult-self told me to be kind to her, but often my child-self took over and I wasn't. On the day of the wedding, Dad and I had to wait and wait for her to be ready. We arrived after Glenda, and we had to hurry to our places before the bride entered the church. I realised later that Mum was not coping well with her son getting married. Apart from this it was a very happy occasion, and I was Master of Ceremonies at the reception.

I decided to fly to Cairns and visit my many friends up north before moving to Melbourne. I so enjoyed remembering the good times of the past. While I felt at peace, I couldn't avoid worrying a little about how I was going to manage financially until my job at Ridley started. I kept reminding myself how, up to this time, God had amazingly provided for me. When my Subaru had died, Judy Walker, the friend whose husband Tony was killed in the Granville train disaster, had given me a Toyota wagon.

Soon after I returned to Booval, my dear friend from Peru, Nancy Black, arrived to stay. She brought me upsetting news of Unión Bíblica, and I was especially distressed to hear that my car, the gift from Scripture Union Australia, had not been looked after. We set out together to drive to Melbourne. Travelling down the coast road, Nancy had a chance to see a variety of scenery—she particularly enjoyed the coastal greenery, such a contrast to the desert in Peru. We called in to see a mutual friend, Joan French, who had been in Peru. I had told her I was bringing someone with me, but when she saw who it was, she was surprised and thrilled. As we talked about Peru, I found myself still grieving that I could not go back.

I got more and more uneasy as we neared Melbourne. I was nervous about so many things: finding somewhere to live, starting my new job on 1 February, finding a church to join, making new friends and catching up with old ones.

I had made my need for a flat known at the Melbourne CMS Summer School and was told on arrival that a place was available in Chapel Street, St Kilda. It was only twenty minutes' drive from Ridley. A man's mother had moved to a nursing home and she wanted to rent out the flat. Nancy and I looked at it on 2 February. It was perfect—in fact, it exceeded my wildest dreams. The two-bedroom ground floor unit had high ceilings and thick brick walls, and I appreciated the fact that the lounge/dining room and my bedroom looked out onto greenery. It was partially furnished, and Barbara Darling and I had fun shopping for what was lacking.

It felt so good to have a place of my own again. In March, when my storage drums from Peru arrived in Melbourne, I was able to make the unit really feel like home.

I was looking forward to being able to entertain again. That opportunity came as early as April, when my sister Debra came from Queensland to stay while she looked for a job and found somewhere to live. Karen came for a weekend—she and her husband, Gavin, had separated. I enjoyed having some fun outings with my sisters.

I visited local churches and decided to join St Paul's Malvern, where I received a warm welcome. I was invited to join a home group, and as I attended services week by week, friendships developed.

Up until my appointment, the Ridley College Bookshop had only had a part-time helper. John Wilson did all the ordering and the shop was two rooms in an old army hut. My first job was to work with John to set up the bookshop in a new building. I was to say where the shelves were to go, but I was thankful John had some ideas. Together we moved the books into place. It was a huge, tiring task, and we worked with a band of helpers on Saturday mornings as well as all the week.

John talked to me about his various involvements and invited me to become a committee member of the Australian Christian Literature Society (ACLS). ACLS supported the overseas publishing and training consultancies of co-founder Kevin Engel, raised funds for projects he identified and organised the Australian Christian Book of the Year awards.

All the newness of everything and everybody was challenging. My workload at the bookshop grew as more and more students came to ask advice and buy books. The vicar of St Paul's Malvern, Graeme Rutherford, his wife, Caroline, and their five children received me into their home with warmth and friendship, and I started to become more involved in the church. Graeme lectured part-time at the college and we often travelled together. He invited me to preach and lead a home group. I had meetings to attend at night, and when I was to preach or speak at a CMS or SU function, I needed time for preparation. Bit by bit my life was in danger of becoming over-busy again. I started not sleeping well, and I often felt I didn't have enough time for shopping and housework. I began to feel again that I was not coping, but as before I covered it up.

In December 1984, when college closed, I did a full stocktake, so I could not go to Queensland for Christmas. My sister Toni and her husband and children spent Christmas Day with me as they were heading for a holiday in Adelaide. They suggested I have a break on the Sunshine Coast in their home while they were away, and this I did, driving up with my friend Marianne Wise. At Toni's home I had time alone and looked back on my first year in Melbourne. I thought, with great thankfulness, of the friendship and support of the Rutherford family and the opportunities Graeme had given me to preach and teach. They had moved to St John's Camberwell and I had remained at St Paul's, but our friendship had continued and I still felt almost part of their family. I valued my friends and groups at St Paul's too.

My thoughts about how I had handled things at the bookshop were not so positive. For the first few months, apart from John, who was my advisor and supporter, two students helped me part-time. As things got busier, it was suggested I hire a full-time assistant. John and I interviewed applicants for the job and together selected Karina Coogan. At first she and I settled into working together reasonably well, but as time went on, I found myself reacting negatively to her suggestions, and to her. I realised I was still threatened by anyone who could quietly and efficiently get on with a job. Karina did this, and I would get unreasonably angry if she made a mistake. I knew I should not revert to old life patterns, yet I did.

I felt I was messing things up again. Sitting there on the Sunshine Coast, I prayed as I looked forward to the year ahead: "Father, walk with me into 1985 in my relationships. Help me to relate in love, in genuine, open concern for others, taking risks, being open and 'real'. Walk with me into the bookshop, give me wisdom and sensitivity. Help me to build others up, particularly Karina."

After two lovely weeks in Queensland, Marianne and I headed south again, making the trip part of our holiday by visiting the Warrumbungle Ranges and Dubbo Zoo. Back in Melbourne, Peter Corney, the director of a new Ridley College youth ministry course, invited me to be involved, and I jumped at the chance—not realising I was still looking for acceptance and recognition.

Already one or two students had talked over some personal problems with me, and each seemed to appreciate the Bible-based help I had given them. I felt that this, along with Bible teaching, was where my gifts lay. I accepted every offer I could to speak, preach or lead study groups. Both CMS and Scripture Union gave me opportunities to speak to large groups. All of these, and especially the lecturing, involved much time for preparation. I was often very nervous speaking to large numbers, but, as so many told me, the people listening felt blessed. I felt I should take every opportunity to be used and rarely refused an invitation. Once again, I was doing too much, getting overtired and not sleeping well, but was afraid to let anyone know.

In 1985 the annual Christian Booksellers' Convention was held in Adelaide, and I decided to go. I arranged to stay with with my sister Karen and her new boyfriend, David. I felt a real pang of the old jealousy towards Karen because she had so quickly entered another relationship after divorcing Gavin. I wondered why I could not find someone for myself.

My chief interest at the convention was theological books. Don Holmes, a friend from Ridley, suggested that if I was in Adelaide for something to do with books, I'd be likely to come across his friend Len Woodley, an Adelaide bookseller, and should introduce myself. I did. Len was a speaker at one of the sessions. I found his talk excellent, and, since the convention was to be in Victoria in 1986 and I would be responsible for the educational books area, I asked him for a copy of his notes. We spoke for less than a minute, but I liked the quality of the man and decided I would ask him to be on my speaker's team the next year.

My parents came to stay with me for a while in November. They were heading to Adelaide to stay with Karen. They were shocked to find I didn't have a television, so they bought me a second-hand one. Dad installed it and they settled down to enjoy it. I found I didn't actually watch it much after they left.

By December I was very tired. Emotions surfaced and I found myself crying a lot. Leaving Peru still hurt so much. I headed for Queensland for Christmas and a holiday, and returned in 1986 determined, with God's help, to be open and honest with Karina as we worked together.

I enjoyed seeing my Melbourne family, the Rutherfords, again. I frequently went to their place after church on a Sunday and would take the children out for picnics to do fun things in the afternoon. This gave Graeme and Caroline a little time to themselves. In the evenings I was often able to talk over how I was struggling in various areas. Their prayerful wisdom and advice about my relationship with Karina was a help. Graeme once said to me, "I have never met anyone who knew their Bible so well and could challenge and encourage others, yet who didn't believe God's promises for herself." I have never forgotten this.

The Victorian committee organising the 1986 Christian Booksellers' Convention chose Albury as the venue, believing it would be easy for members from other states to reach. I invited Len Woodley from Adelaide; he delivered two seminars on bookselling, and all were delighted with his input. I lent him my car so he could get around until he had to catch the plane home. When I collected it, I found a brief note of thanks, and an apology for mangling one of my favourite cassettes.

Back in the bookshop, Karina and I were still having difficulties working together. I knew how much I needed God's grace and I prayed much about our relationship. We had some counselling together. This helped a little and somehow enabled us to manage together.

TWENTY-SEVEN

El Salvador and Peru

I was at work in Ridley College Bookshop in October 1986 when I was surprised by a phone call from Paul Clark in Peru. He asked me to come to El Salvador in December to be guest speaker at a Unión Bíblica training conference on camping. He explained that funds were available for my trip.

I was amazed that Paul believed I had something to contribute. It went a long way to balance my previous conception of absolute failure.

I cried out to God for guidance, and talked to John Wilson and Barbara Darling. Both felt I should go. Earlier in the year, I had written down words I felt God was saying to me: "I will restore you to your family, and set you aside for service. You will be a light as you have never been before. Do not be hasty. Wait for the Lord."

The academic year concluded in November, and we did an early stocktake at the bookshop so I could depart Australia on 27 November. Two friends drove me to the airport, and the Rutherfords, with their two youngest, were there to see me off. My suitcase was too heavy, and it was good to have friends to help me buy another one and book it through. I was so pleased to have the chance to revisit South America, remembering how miserable I had felt when I did this trip in reverse after being sent home.

In California I was met by Lois Dodds once again and spent three nights at her Ventura home. When we first got there, I opened the new suitcase and discovered it wasn't mine. We phoned the airport, took the case back and collected the right one. Lois was to speak at a conference in Los Angeles the next day, so I went with her. We talked about my situation and she suggested I do a Myers-Briggs personality test while I was with them. I found out I was what the Myers-Briggs system described as INFP—a personality that is borderline extrovert and introvert, intuitive, more reliant on feelings than thinking, and perceptive rather than judgmental. This was a lightbulb moment. I began to see why I had ended up involved with far more than just the bookshop.

On 1 December I went by bus back to Los Angeles. My flight for El Salvador didn't leave until 11.10 pm, so I had time to see Norm and Susie Hoffman and thank them for caring for me three years before. I was nervous about this final leg of the journey, wondering how well my Spanish would be understood and how I would get through customs, especially as I had come without a visa.

I arrived in San Salvador, El Salvador's capital, at 3.30 pm on 2 December. There was only a minor hiccup at customs—I was warned not to come again without a visa and it took a very long time to get my bags. I was met by Jorge Flores, General Secretary of Unión Bíblica in El Salvador. He drove me to the home of the Vegus family where I was to stay. The heat, the noise and the modesty of the house were not easy to deal with. A bed (with mattress, pillow and sheet) and my case were all that fitted into my room. After a brief rest, I was taken out to tea, but I ate very little because the traditional *pupusas* we ordered were very fatty.

I was surprised at how cold it was at night. I slept in my tracksuit for warmth—or rather, tried to sleep, with little success. The noise of cars and trucks—seemingly without mufflers—and of someone typing in the next room, kept me awake for hours.

I was up early in the morning and ready to go out to breakfast with members of an evangelical church that had organised a three-day seminar. I was to speak at this church before the Unión Bíblica training camp. After breakfast I was taken on a tour of the city. I was shocked to see the terrible effects of the earthquake that had struck San Salvador two months before. There were buildings where the first few floors had collapsed like a pack of cards, and I was told story after story of lives lost.

I had been warned before coming that the water was not safe to drink because the pipes had ruptured during the earthquake. I was constantly thirsty, so rather than drinking the water, I ate the pulp of the local *maracuya* (a large, yellow passionfruit).

Jorge Flores.
1986

It was arranged that I should meet Mardoqueo Carranza, chairman of the Unión Bíblica Committee in El Salvador, and his family on my last day before the seminar. He picked me up in his car and parked around the corner from his home. He then rang his front doorbell rather than use a key. Once inside, he explained that he had to park away from the house so that he could see if anyone was following him, and he didn't carry keys so that if he was detained, no one could get into his house. There were certainly security issues in El Salvador.

After a nice lunch, a young couple showed me more of San Salvador. I saw much of the poor part of the city as well as the more prosperous. The couple were keen to be involved in camps and asked me a lot of questions. I had so little time on my own to read my Bible and pray, so I was thankful others were praying for me.

The seminar went better than I dared to hope. Being immersed in Spanish, I found my fluency returned. I had twelve hours to fill, so, as well as teaching, I gave my listeners plenty of practical tasks and taught them games. These were all new experiences for them. The concept of small group work was, for most, a very forward-thinking idea. On the last day, the participants helped plan the leaders' training camp to be held the following week, which quite a few of them would be attending. I based my material largely on what I had done in Peru. The practical application of the theory was to be experienced at the camp.

I was pleased to have a day between the seminar and the camp in which to show my appreciation to the Vegus family by taking them out to lunch. I was exhausted by this stage and slept soundly on that final night. I met the campers the next day. Jorge was camp director; I was there just to help where needed. We couldn't travel far, so our "campsite" was a house on a coffee plantation, not far from town. The house had been damaged in the earthquake and everyone had to sleep on a concrete-floored verandah, the leaders sleeping between the boys and the girls. I was glad I had an airbed with me. The conditions were primitive.

I led one or two Bible studies at the beginning, then encouraged Jorge to try out the new things he had learnt at the seminar. He became more confident as the week went on. During my time in San Salvador

I had seen many poverty-stricken people and I realised that Jorge himself, a teacher, lived in a very small house and had no hope of ever getting a car or telephone. He worked tirelessly to tell others about Jesus and knew he could die for his faith, but his one longing was that others would see Jesus in him. His life was a real challenge to me.

Two young soldiers, weapons at their side, watched everything we did. They were there to protect us from possible attack. On the last night of the camp, I woke hearing gunfire very close. Everyone else slept through it. I lay awake wondering what would happen next. Would I die? In the morning I heard there had been a skirmish on a nearby ridge.

I had two days after the end of the camp before I was to go to Peru. I visited the cathedral where Archbishop Oscar Romero had been murdered only five years earlier. I did a little shopping and met with another group of eighteen- to twenty-five-year-olds, whom I spoke to and encouraged. I felt enormously privileged to have had the opportunity to come to El Salvador and hoped I had been able to teach the people well. I knew how much I had learnt from them.

My plane left at 6.50 p.m. and took me to Peru via Panama. During my twenty-hour stopover in Panama I visited the Canal and was amazed to see huge ships navigating the narrow stretch of water. I arrived in Lima in the morning and was met by Berenice, Paul, Marty and three others. It was wonderful to see them.

As the days went by and we visited old sites such as Chaclacayo and Kawai, I somehow knew that I no longer had a place there. The young people I had been close to were now either married or engaged. I visited quite a few in their homes. I met with several committees and encouraged them in their work. I spent Christmas Day with the Clarks and their twenty-six guests. On other days I visited friends. I was thankful that they felt confident enough to share some of their problems with me. Some also talked about their role in what had happened to me three years before. I knew it was important that they see I was now okay. Quite a few had been traumatised by my sudden departure.

During my visit, Paul also talked to me at length about the possibility of my starting Unión Bíblica in Ecuador. He encouraged me to consider this prayerfully when I returned to Australia.

Friends saw me off at the airport and I set off for Chile and Argentina. I went first to Santiago to visit Gaye Mercier. The view of the Andes from the plane was spectacular. A bus took me to Parque Los Heroes (Park of the Heroes) where Gaye met me, and we took a taxi to her home. It was important for me to thank Gaye for all she had done for me in the months before I left Peru. I assured her that God had overruled and brought good for me out of those very difficult days. She admitted that there were things about my departure that she would now handle differently. Gaye took me by cable car to the top of Cerro San Cristobal, where I looked down through a telescope at the vast city of Santiago. I felt this was a healing time together.

The purpose of my trip to Buenos Aires was to meet Beatriz Buono, who was to come to Australia for the next Christian Booksellers' Conference in June 1987. I also had a quick visit with John and Gayelene Harrower, CMS missionaries who were soon to return to Australia. Beatriz was to replace John as the director of Certeza, an Argentine Christian publisher and bookseller. We shared deeply. She told me how she had become a follower of Jesus Christ through the testimony of a fellow science student in her second year at university. I knew I would enjoy her visit to Australia. In just two days we became close friends.

My next flight was to Miami, where I was able to spend three happy days with my Peruvian friend Jackie in a cottage she had rented at a beautiful location by the water in Florida Keys. She had married, but I did not meet her husband or see her home. She talked of her confusion about who she was because her mother had told her that it was her unmarried aunt who had actually given birth to her. Somehow, as she shared this with me, I understood for myself that I no longer depended on others for my identity, as I had done in the past. I left feeling I would probably not see Jackie again.

On my flight home from Honolulu, I was surprised to meet Maurice Betteridge, the principal of Ridley College, and his wife, Jacquie, on their way home from sabbatical leave. Reflecting on my trip back to South America, I realised how important it had been. I had said goodbye and established new relationships with those I had known in the past. It had been a key chapter in my growth.

Leadership training, El Salvador. 1986

Lesley and Beatriz visit Adelaide.
1987

TWENTY-EIGHT

Bombshell two

By mid-January 1987 I was back in the bookshop, praying that I could work well with Karina. Within three weeks of my return, I was surprised to be called by Maurice Betteridge to his office. He told me I was no longer wanted in the bookshop. He asked me to write a letter of resignation immediately or he would have to sack me.

I knew I had failed, time and time again, to be patient, and now it was too late to try again. I walked out of the office in a daze and wandered down the street trying to take this in. I somehow knew I had never been really happy with the bookshop work—it was my lecturing and contact with students that I felt happiest doing. Nonetheless, my sense of failure was overwhelming.

I wrote my letter: "Recently I have become increasingly aware that I am frustrated by my work in the bookshop. I would like leave until the end of February, subsequent to which I resign. Regretfully …" Maurice was defensive but reacted positively to my letter, affirmed all I had contributed to the Ridley community and gave me a warm hug. I contacted a few of the students I knew and told them of my decision to leave. They were understandably surprised.

I rang Michael Corbett-Jones and arranged to see him. He felt this development may mean that more of my past pain could be resolved. To me it felt like the same pain I experienced when I left Peru. Close friends were supportive and stayed with me for a few days. I had some encouraging letters from students expressing their thanks and disappointment that I was leaving. The Ridley staff also expressed surprise but accepted it as my decision. They had a morning tea for me and gave me a briefcase as a farewell gift.

I caught a bus to Sydney to see Michael. I stayed with Don and Margaret again. My parents were on their way south for a holiday so I arranged to travel back to Melbourne with them. We took a leisurely three days driving down the coast, staying a night at both Merimbula and Lakes Entrance.

Mum and Dad expressed surprise that I had left the bookshop. I couldn't talk to them about my real situation, nor about my unsure future. Much had been resolved between us, but I still did not have an open relationship with them. I noticed that Mum seemed unwell, but I did not know why. On this trip I realised that leaving the bookshop was actually good for me, liberating me from the straightjacket of trying to be what I was not. I was, however, anxious about finding work.

Beatriz Buono arrived in March, and I was encouraged by John Wilson (now a bishop) to drive her to Sydney via Adelaide so that my Spanish could be a backup for her if she had trouble with her English. She was keen to visit Australian bookshops and publishers. Having visited the Melbourne centres, we took two days to enjoy the Great Ocean Road to South Australia. I told her of my resignation and my hurt and anger at how it had come about. She understood and affirmed me.

In Adelaide we stayed with my sister Karen and visited bookshops. Len Woodley and his senior colleague took us out to lunch. Then we headed north towards Sydney through the Barossa Valley. Beatriz was amazed to see vines growing so close to the road that she could pick some grapes. I took her to Jenolan Caves and across the Blue Mountains. An enduring friendship was forged on this trip.

In Sydney Beatriz went to stay with Kevin and Dorothy Engel while I stayed with Felicity Fries. I had a number of counselling sessions with Michael. He pointed out that I had not yet learnt how to give and take. I always acted either as the child or the parent in my relationships. I knew Beatriz had helped me to know I could love unconditionally. I felt so thankful for her.

So that I could monitor my pattern of behaviour in my next job, Michael encouraged me to prepare a "Recipe for Disaster". He said I could follow this recipe and fail again, or I could choose not to follow it and succeed. I was challenged by my Bible reading in Philippians: "In humility value others above yourselves, not looking to your own interests but each of you to the interest of the others" (2:3–4 NIV). I prayed, "Help me relax in your power and allow your love to flow through me. Help me to live in your victory."

Education officer with CMS Victoria.
1987

TWENTY-NINE

Wider horizons

Within a short time of returning to Melbourne, I had three positions to consider: the Ecuador one, offered by Paul Clark; one with CMS Victoria, to be responsible for deputations and promotion; and one for a promotional role with Scripture Union Victoria. I accepted the CMS position and was commissioned as CMS Victoria Education Officer on 7 May 1987, at St Paul's Malvern. Bishop John Wilson preached and CMS Victoria's General Secretary, Edwin Lang, assisted by Graeme Rutherford, conducted the commissioning. Many friends were there. I spent the day fasting and seeking God and felt truly encouraged.

The CMS Autumn School was held at the end of May, and I was involved in the missionary presentations. In planning for missionaries to speak, I was able to use my experience with Unión Bíblica, and many senior school students were challenged to consider serving God as missionaries after their tertiary training.

After the "high" of this time, I went home tired and dispirited, feeling very alone. I had spoken sixteen times in six weeks as well as visiting and entertaining numerous people. I had a celebration rally in June to plan for, an audio-visual to prepare for synod and the 1988 Summer School to organise. I found it hard to take time off. I was so unsure of myself and feared failure with every event. But I kept praying, and God answered. Each event went off well.

Although my new job was demanding, it was also very fulfilling. I felt privileged to meet missionaries coming home on furlough and seeing new missionaries off to their new work. I was able to make creative changes to deputation work, Summer School planning and CMS publicity and promotion material. I used my "day off" (when I could take it) to keep in touch with friends. Barbara Darling and I had a couple of days away together, and I had a lovely trip to Queensland to attend my brother Ian's ordination and speak at my brother Andrew's marriage to Donna. I spent Christmas with Ian and Glenda in Dalby, where Ian was a curate. Their first child, Amelia Rae, was born while I was still in Queensland. I was staying with Toni and Gary, so I was able to see my new niece before returning to Victoria.

Back in Melbourne, I was excited to receive a message from Len Woodley saying he was coming across from Adelaide and would like to visit me. I discovered he liked rhubarb, so I prepared some for him. As he ate, he shared with me some of his issues. I prayed for him and he left. I found him easy to talk to and we were obviously becoming good friends.

Because I felt so alone, on one of my days off I listed fifteen qualities I would "require" in a husband. I found this helpful because it stopped me seeing every man I met as a potential spouse. I knew too that I had much to learn so that I could really be myself. Graeme Rutherford helped me with this. One day I said to him, "I am just the CMS Education Officer." He corrected me and said, "You should say, 'I am the CMS Education Officer.'" Removing one word altered how I saw myself.

Len came again to Melbourne for the 1987 Australian Booksellers' Association Conference and again we spent time together. Karen and David planned to marry in Adelaide early in the new year and she suggested I come with a partner. I tentatively contacted Len and asked if he would go with me to the wedding on 5 January. At home in Booval for Christmas, I received his reply. Yes, he would be happy to join me. I was so pleased.

THIRTY
Moving west

After Christmas Mum and Dad set off to drive to Adelaide. I stayed in Queensland to catch up with friends, then flew to Adelaide on the morning of the wedding. Dad picked me up at the airport and drove me to Karen's home. Later in the day, Len collected my parents and me and drove us to the place where both the marriage and reception were to be held.

Karen and David had asked me to speak at the ceremony. I based my talk on Colossians 3:12–17, focusing on the need for forgiveness to be the hallmark of the love they shared as they let the peace of God rule in their lives together.

When the dancing started at the reception, Len suggested we go for a walk. He said he wanted to show me his grandfather's former home. As we walked, we became aware of how much we had in common. He had to leave to take my parents and Karen's children back to where they were staying while Karen and David were on their honeymoon, but afterwards he came back and picked me up. He took me to a lovely spot overlooking the waters of St Vincent Gulf, and we sat and talked and prayed until the early hours of the morning. At one point, Len prayed, "If you mean us to come together, show us the way." I was already conscious that Len ticked off most of the fifteen points on my "requirements for a husband" list, and by the time I arrived home at 4 am, about to fly back to Melbourne the next day, I felt our relationship was changing—though by how much I wasn't sure.

Back in Melbourne and trying to get on with my job, I found I couldn't get Len out of my thoughts. I had been thrown into a loop by what we'd shared. I knew I wanted to get to know him more; I knew too that I longed for a partner who I could share with day by day. I wrote to him and told him I was finding it hard to concentrate. He rang and helped me get my feet back on the ground. A few days later, he rang again to say he had decided to come to the Melbourne CMS Summer School.

I met him at the airport, and together we met Samuel and Lily Escobar, who were to be speakers at the school. As I drove my three passengers to their places of residence, Lily asked me in Spanish who Len was. I said, "He's a friend I'm getting to know." I left Len at Ridley where he was to stay. As I was about to drive away, he handed a sheet of paper and said, "Here are some of my jottings for you to peruse." I was overcome with joy when I read what he had written. It showed me how well he could express himself, his desire to be God's person and what he would look for in a wife. He said that any future partner he had would need to be someone with whom he could serve God. I wrote back saying that I resonated positively with all he had written.

The Summer School was a busy time for me. It was a success beyond my wildest dreams. I thanked God from the bottom of my heart. Five hundred and sixty people attended. The theme highlighted how Christian missionaries had to be aware of their social responsibilities as they shared the message of Jesus.

When all the conference packing up was finished, Len came back to my apartment and joined me in a simple tea. He returned the next morning and we shared deeply. We both had failed in a number of areas and talked about these things. Len knew the grace of God's forgiveness. His Christian walk had not been one of triumph but of coping with life's traumas. He did not talk piously, and I suspect he was more honest than I was. He told me about a lady friend he had in Adelaide, explaining that he would have to sort out that relationship before committing to me. I knew I loved him, but I had to trust that God would enable me to accept whatever decisions he came to. I told him that I would find it hard if he decided to marry his Adelaide girlfriend, but of course I would let him go. I knew, if he made that choice, it would be because he really believed it to be God's will.

Len stayed in my apartment while I went to Katoomba for the CMS Missionaries' Conference. The evening before leaving, I introduced him to the Myers-Briggs test that had produced such a significant insight for me. It was new to him, and I was fascinated to find that his personality type was one labelled ENTJ, signifying an extrovert with intuitive thinking and judging. This was a revelation to Len, and it profoundly affected his understanding of himself and others. My type, INFP, was defined as "idealist"; his was defined as "commandant"!

When I returned from Katoomba, I found, laid out on my bed, an exquisite hand-painted silk scarf and a beautiful letter saying, "The riches of the colours capture for me the richness of our friendship."

Len's birthday was in February, so I sent him a small Peruvian leather coaster on which I inscribed Philippians 1:9–11. I phoned him in the evening. This call left me with a sinking feeling. He explained to me that he was not in a position to be more than friends. He needed to free himself from his lady friend and make sure there was no possibility of reconciling with his former wife, Judy. I tried, tearfully, to accept that Len and I would never marry, but when he came to Melbourne a few weeks later, he stayed with me in my unit, me sleeping on the couch and him in my bed. I constantly battled between praying that God would bring us together in marriage and that God's will would be done for us both.

I found myself writing to him several times a week, and he wrote back or phoned, though less often. I asked him whether he still held hands with his girlfriend and he was a bit evasive. He did, however, start to talk to me about his daughter, Heather, and how he had helped her with her homework and found a "work experience" job for her. He was seeing less of his lady friend, and told me she had said, "If you are going to let me go, please do it gently."

In March Len wrote to tell me he had talked at length with Jason Page, a minister at the church he attended, Holy Trinity Adelaide, about his failures in life. Jason was shocked, and it was I who had to assure Len that the freedom of forgiveness he showed was an indication of the healing and wholeness that had come to him.

Over the next months, I noticed Len took every opportunity he could to come to Melbourne and spend time with me. I knew I loved him, but Graeme Rutherford challenged me about whether I was prepared, if it was God's will, to be always single. I tried to think "yes", but deep down I knew I wanted to be Len's wife. He drew out the best in me. Knowing him also gave me a fresh insight into my childhood experiences. I had believed I was a replacement in my parents' eyes, but I was also an agent of healing.

Len wrote me many long emails, sharing deeply. In one he said, "I think, Lesley, basically I have wanted and needed to be confronted with God's real Love. Quite simply, he has done that through you. God does know what that has cost you. The more I think of it, the more it is awesome … I love you, Lesley, and I want that love always to build you up and never deflect you from his purpose … Every day I thank God for the privilege of knowing you and the gift of your love and friendship."

Over the months that followed, I continued to swing between thinking our friendship was leading to marriage and resigning myself that it was not to be. I went through a period of believing that, because Len was divorced, I should not marry him. I read a lot of books on marriage from a biblical perspective and concluded that the sin of divorce was no worse than any other sin. Len had acknowledged and confessed his sin and was forgiven. One day he unexpectedly sent me a desk lamp which was identical to one he bought for himself, with a card bringing together 1 John and the thought of light and love sharpening vision. I had attended a journaling workshop and was able to express the ups and downs in my feelings in writing.

In June 1988, my work with CMS took me to Adelaide to preach and speak at a number of venues. Len took me out several times. On the Saturday night, we went to a performance of the Adelaide Symphony Orchestra, and I was amazed to find our seats were in A-Reserve. After I preached at a CMS service at St George's Magill, Len took me for a walk in one of his favourite places, the nearby Morialta Falls. On our way back, we encountered a number of CMS members doing the same walk, and knew our cover had been well and truly blown. On this trip I was asked to apply for the position of CMS General Secretary in Adelaide, but I decided not to.

The eighteenth of July 1988 was my fortieth birthday. The Rutherfords organised a splendid birthday party for me with thirty-five friends at The Cuckoo restaurant in the Dandenong Ranges. I asked Len if he would like to come over from Adelaide and he said yes. After the main course, I opened the many generous gifts I had received.

Len's was a large rectangular package. I unwrapped it to a communal intake of breath: it was an original Pro Hart painting, done as a book jacket for one of Len's friends, Geoffrey Bingham. (Later Len joked with our friends that the only way he could get it back was to marry me!) I had hoped that there would be clarification about our relationship that night, but there was none.

My parents' gift was the cost of a trip to Brisbane in August to attend Expo 88, part of Australia's bicentennial celebrations. Len decided to join me. I told my family he was just a very close friend. But there was mutual progress in the months that followed, and Len suggested I visit him in Adelaide after Christmas.

I had Christmas lunch, as usual, with the Rutherfords, and then they drove me to the airport. I was excited. I wondered whether I would be engaged to be married or confirmed in my singleness by the time I left Adelaide.

It took until 30 December before Len, sitting with a cup of coffee discussing Scripture passages, suddenly said, "Will you marry me?" I felt numb and said, "Are you really asking? Do you want an answer?" He hesitated, then said quietly, "Yes." I answered in the affirmative. There was no display of emotion. Len departed for Glenelg to see a friend and then had to work at his shop that night and the next day.

On New Year's Day 1989, Jason Page and his wife Ann came over to celebrate our engagement. Jason suggested Len should buy me a ring. But I knew something was wrong—Len was a quivering mess. He had read Paul's discussion of divorce in 1 Corinthians 7 again and felt he was disobeying God. Jason talked with him. On 5 January Jason and Ann came to accompany me at Len's place. We played pool while Len went to visit Judy again. He was away for over two hours and came back exhausted.

He went into the kitchen, made coffee and carried it into the poolroom. Taking a sip, he looked at me and said, "Lesley McGrath, I want to ask you if you will be my wife and come here and make this your home." I couldn't speak. Jason said, "Tell him yes!" I said, "Yes! Yes!", and we embraced. Jason went back to hitting balls on the pool table.

We decided to marry on 18 March.

Wedding, Holy Trinity, Adelaide.
1989

THIRTY-ONE
New vistas

Having settled the date, we went together to choose an engagement ring. It was flat with two rows of tiny rubies and three rows of small diamonds on each side. It had to be altered to fit my finger, so Len said he would bring it to Melbourne for the 1989 CMS Summer School in March. That gave me time to carry out my responsibilities for the conference and give CMS notice.

Because of his divorce, Len had to get special permission from the archbishop to marry in the Anglican Church. This was granted, so we asked Jason to marry us at Holy Trinity. The date was booked.

Wedding invitations had to be printed. We had not found a venue for our reception, so we simply invited our two hundred guests to a buffet lunch—destination unknown. We booked rooms at a motel in Kent Town for our interstate guests. After hunting around, we were very pleased to book a lunch reception at the College Arms Hotel, only a short walk from Holy Trinity.

Back in Melbourne, with Jill Wilson's help, I bought an elegant wedding dress made of soft, gentle, falling crepe material. I had some people tell me I should not be marrying Len, but by now I was sure it was God's will. Others encouraged me with their enthusiasm and congratulations. I took time to write down nine detailed "Goals of Our Marriage", ending with: "Summary Goal? To glorify God and enjoy him forever, together humbly submissive by his grace." I didn't realise then how much I had to learn, nor how difficult this learning would be.

I flew to South Australia the week before The Day. My four sisters, all by then in Adelaide, helped me get Len's home ready to show interstate visitors on the morning of the wedding. I wanted people to see where we would be living, and I had bought a green and white silk dress and crystal beads to wear for the showing. I had arranged for this to take place between 9.30 and 10.30 am so I had time to change for our midday wedding service.

My father picked me up to drive me to the church. I suggested we pray together before we leave. He said a few words and tears began to stream down his face, so I finished the prayer. On the way to the service, he told me about his concern for Mum's health. I persuaded him to seek medical help as soon as he arrived home.

I didn't have bridesmaids as I had invited my three nieces, one nephew and the five Rutherford children to accompany Dad and me down the aisle. Dad's job was to hand me over to Len.

The service was all we could have asked for. Len and I took communion together as our first act as a married couple. Alan Washington sang two solos, one of which his wife Alison had written especially for us. The words "When she came into my life, you were there, you were there, Shepherd of my life" captured the basis of our relationship in Jesus. My engagement ring became my wedding ring, with "Len and Lesley 18.3.1989" inscribed on it.

The reception was great. In his speech Dad joked, "I have told Lesley not to work herself out of a job this time!" Len and I didn't eat much. We had family photos taken at about 4 pm, then Ian drove us to Len's car. We changed in the darkness of the carpark, dropped in at a chemist to get Len some medication (he had not felt well during the day) and set off down the old South Eastern Highway towards Naracoorte. Len drove all the way. This perplexed me, but I didn't mention it till later. I just kept thanking God for giving me Len as a partner.

I discovered new things about Len on our honeymoon. He liked to watch *Sesame Street* before setting out anywhere in the morning and wanted to be home at night in time to watch *Dr Who*. He cared very much about how I looked. My sports' shoes were shabby and he sent me off to buy new ones.

Back home in Grandview Grove, Toorak Gardens, I found we had much to learn about relating to one another. Our sleep patterns were different—Len was an early riser; I was a late-to-bed, late-to-rise person. Len was particular where things were kept and that they should always be in that place. I struggled to learn to live this way.

Words were of great importance to Len, yet when I said to him, "Len, I need you to tell me you love me," he replied, "I've told you once and I'll tell you if I change my mind!" This actually provided me with a great sense of security—when he did tell me, it took on a special significance.

In May, Len's mother, Margaret, turned seventy and we had a party for her at home. We worked hard together to clean the house, and I could not believe how particular Len was. He even cleaned the ceilings. Slow as I was, and completely dependent on recipe books, I prepared the food for the party. Thanks to Len's careful preparation, it was a great success.

Buenos Aires.
1991

THIRTY-TWO

... and new challenges!

By mid-June I was finding it hard that we never seemed to have time to talk together. Len was too tired when he came home from work and I was not much good in the mornings. It took years before we found a compromise "chatting time" at 10.30 am morning tea.

In those early months, I knew I had to learn to be more organised. I asked Len to tell me what he expected of his wife. He decided to put it in writing. He firstly reinforced his desire to fulfil the nine points of love and service to God that I had written when we became engaged, adding, "I want us to participate in things God calls us to together, and to make each other fully free to participate in things that we do best personally." Then he outlined further expectations in detail.

> This has implications for housework and household organisation. I want our home to be a haven of calmness, a refuge from the busyness of work, a place of restoration and replenishment. For me that includes a place which is clean, tidy and quiet ... I'd love it to be normal, when I come home, for you to be calm and relaxed yourself (sitting down even!) to welcome me into such an environment—sit me down with a drink and possibly chat about nothing in particular—then sit down to a meal that magically appears without stress and bustle and tension; helping you to get dishes out of the way, then get on with the evening activities, at home or out or whatever they happen to be. For me that is totally destroyed if there are chores hanging about to be done ... For me housework is like accountancy. It is not the prime purpose of the house or the business—it's a simple and essential chore which, if done proficiently

and professionally, aids the entire household or business to be what it ought to be.

Len then suggested a detailed program that would enable me to have the basic chores done by 11.30 am, suggesting that I then do early preparations for dinner. He asked that I try to sit and relax, perhaps listening to music, for the half hour before he was due to come home so I could offer him the quiet peace he valued. He also suggested I program times in the afternoons to write letters, relax gardening or go shopping, so that Tuesdays could be kept utterly free for us to be together and Thursdays free for me.

In late July I received my next written message. It must have been a bad evening.

> I hated coming in tonight and finding I couldn't have a quick lie down because there were no pillowcases on the bed; then couldn't have a game of pool because the pool table was covered with washing; then, needing to spit to clear my throat, finding the sink full of dishes; then going to do something else and finding the vacuum cleaner in the middle of the floor, a broom propped up against the wall and yet another pile of papers and letters on the kitchen table.

He continued to list things he couldn't do, then said, "There are 'reasons' for most of these things, but most of them are not valid. It is a combination of either inefficient or untidy work habits … The bad habits can be changed quite simply." He listed four faults that caused the problems, adding that "inefficient people quite often PLAN THEIR WORK but don't follow through with the second part, which is to WORK THEIR PLAN." Four good habits he listed were:

> 1. Do the most consuming and least enjoyable chore first, allowing no distraction.

> 2. Do not commence a task without first assembling the tools, utensils or ingredients required to see the task completed.

3. Once a task is commenced—see it through to completion.

4. If completion is impossible—don't leave it. REPLACE the tools and reassemble them when the opportunity to complete the task arises.

This was the reality of living with an ENTJ 'commandant'! While I reacted to his criticism of the way I operated, I saw wisdom in what he wrote. Over the years, I went on to put many of his ideas into practice in my own way. Certainly, the early days of our marriage were a learning experience for both of us.

With Len.
1993

THIRTY-THREE

Life changes again

My parents had expressed pleasure that I was marrying a businessman with a stable business. Within five months of our marriage, at the August directors' meeting of Len's company, Standard Book, it was decided to ask the bank for the usual annual overdraft to fund the purchase of textbooks for the coming academic year. Len was astounded at their refusal. He was confused and depressed that night, and woke the next morning, sat up in bed and said, "I don't want to work in retail anymore."

The bank had suggested he mortgage our house for the loan. I was thankful that, after prayer, Len said that was not an option.

We prayed together for a solution before he left as usual for the shop. He had previously considered, but not explored, a partnership with the Sydney-based Dymocks, and just an hour later, John Forsyth, the managing director of Dymocks, rang to invite himself to coffee with Len. En route from Coolgardie to Sydney, a pilots' strike had left him unexpectedly stranded in Adelaide. The meeting was relaxed as they discussed a possible partnership arrangement.

A few days later, Len chanced to meet a friend, Jim Crawford, who was enthusiastic about Standard Book. This led to Jim offering an alternative option to the Dymock's one.

In mid-October 1989 Len and I looked prayerfully at the four options he had. We could borrow against our home; join with Jim Crawford in Adelaide; accept Dymock's offer to buy fifty or fifty-five per cent; or sell one hundred per cent to them. Len realised that whether it was fifty per cent or one hundred per cent, Dymocks would call the tune. He decided to sell outright to Dymocks.

Len had just turned fifty, and after more than twenty-five years at Standard Book, he was ready for a change. Grant Octoman, a friend and accountant, flew with him to Sydney for the negotiations. They were tough, but having the alternative Crawford offer in hand greatly assisted the outcome. Negotiations were finalised on 1 November 1989, with Len appointed to manage the transition on a two-year contract.

Len's dream was to have a modest income with time for reflection, reading and writing. He wanted to encourage Christians to read well-chosen secular books as well as Christian ones. He felt he could do this without owning a bookshop.

Dymocks were not interested in the two other arms of Len's business, Standard Book's second-hand section and ALS, a library supply company. ALS was already separately located, so our first task was to find a new home for the second-hand bookshop. Len found a first-floor location at 6A Rundle Mall and supervised a superb renovation of the shop, with a unique colour scheme. It was a mammoth task moving the books—packing them in boxes, transporting them to the mall and lifting them, with mechanical help, through the first-floor windows. Then the boxes had to be carried to the shop, unpacked and shelved. We worked late into the night before the official opening.

The shop was renamed Adelaide Booksellers. I felt a part of this enterprise and enjoyed going to see how it was progressing. As I so often did, I overdid things, and Len had to suggest I wasn't giving the manager, David Brookman, enough freedom to do his job.

These big business decisions were very demanding on Len, yet he still found time to encourage and support me in my involvement at Holy Trinity. I was asked to give three talks on prayer at a Trinity Women's Day. I was very nervous and, because of the time-consuming bookshop discussions, felt unprepared on the night before I was due to speak. Len calmed me down and helped me with my talks. This was the beginning of a special ministry God gave me at the church.

Len had made sure, before we were married, that I was happy not to have children. He had three already—Jenny, 22, David, 20, and Heather, 18—and felt that was enough to cope with. As time went on, I understood his reasoning. Although all three lived elsewhere, they had grown up in Grandview Grove and still considered it their home. They treated me with courtesy, but I knew it would take time for them to truly accept me. I felt they became more relaxed when I asked them to call me "Lesley".

Jenny had been living with her partner, Steve Avory, for some time, and at Len's surprise fiftieth birthday party, they announced they were expecting a baby. They were living with a friend on a farm at Murdinga, near Cummins on the Eyre Peninsula. David lived in a unit with his partner, Tina; when we visited him, he proudly showed me his thriving crop of cannabis. Heather was living in a unit in Mitchell Park with her partner, Peter. We thought all was well with her, but whenever we visited and knocked, no one answered the door. We learnt later that Heather was being physically and mentally abused. She came to stay with us at about the same time we welcomed Kelly Rose Avory, Len's first grandchild, into the world. I was determined to help Len support his family.

At Holy Trinity I was pleased to have further opportunities to use my gifts to serve God. I met once a week with Colin Sheehan, the clergyman responsible for the weekly 11 am services, to help him plan them. Then the rector, the Revd Reg Piper, asked me to organise and run the Trinity Conference for the following year (1992). Since Len and I were planning a trip to South America for April 1991, I got as much of the conference preparation done as possible done before we left. Reg wanted the emphasis to be on equipping people to share their faith. My conference title, used in the church bulletin as advertising, was "Don't Yell It … Tell It!" Instead of inviting a guest speaker, as was the custom, I suggested that Reg give an introductory talk, followed by workshops. Each workshop leader was asked to come up with an innovative title for their area: three of these were "Vision and Vigour for Viable Visiting", "Making Friends, Changing Lives" and "Become a Secret Agent". Those attending would be able to join three different workshops on the day. Bill Hague worked with me and would be available to lead the conference if anything should happen that meant I couldn't be there.

One possibility was that I would be called to Queensland because of my mother's health. I was distressed to hear from Dad, soon after they returned home from our wedding, that she had bulbar palsy, one of a group of illnesses known as motor neurone diseases. As she became more dependent on Dad, I felt sad that I lived too far away to help him care for her. So I rang some friends at All Saints Booval, and one of them, Joan McLean, organised a roster of people to sit with Mum one afternoon a week. This gave Dad time to have a break to play bowls in Ipswich.

THIRTY-FOUR

Purposeful travel

In early April 1991 Len and I set off on our first trip together to Latin America. Certeza Argentina, the Christian publisher and bookseller led by Beatriz Buono, had requested a consultant to visit from the Australian Christian Literature Society. The ACLS Council asked us to do the visit and provided some financial support.

After the busyness of adjusting to married life, establishing Adelaide Booksellers and (for me) joining a new church, we were ready for this trip. I was looking forward to introducing Len to a part of the world I had learned to love.

The tiring flight from Auckland to Buenos Aires seemed to go on forever. Beatriz met us at Buenos Aires airport and drove us to the Hotel Lancaster. Many South Americans drive erratically and Beatriz hadn't had her licence long, so I was glad Len was in the back seat. He probably had his eyes shut, praying. We showered, relaxed, had an early dinner and a good night's sleep, and were ready to meet Beatriz again next morning. I was pleased I could still speak Spanish well enough to get by.

One of the purposes of the trip, with Len's new ventures in mind, was for him to see how Christian bookshops were managing in South America. When Beatriz did not arrive at the arranged time, Len was concerned. I knew the Latin American concept of time so was not fazed. She arrived almost an hour late, and we sat and chatted for a while before setting off to see the Certeza shop in the city centre, followed by a trip to the office in Wilde. Len chose to sit in the back again and told me he focused on the patterns on the cobbled roads to take his mind off the driving.

The next day we spent time examining Certeza's computer systems and programs with their IT consultant, Jorge Grippo, and visiting other bookshops. After visiting the Certeza shop in Lomas de Zamora the next day, I took Len to see the famous Teatro Colón, acoustically considered to be among the finest opera houses in the world.

On Sunday we travelled by bus to Wilde to go to church with Beatriz. It was good to hear Len singing the Spanish hymns with gusto in English, and Roberto, the pastor, translated Len's welcome and message. After lunch at Beatriz's apartment, we visited a market where the food and produce were set out, Andean style, on the ground. Before dinner (again at Beatriz's apartment), we had a long discussion about Certeza, then dined with Rodolfo Arena, the chairman of Certeza, and his wife, Cecilia. Len and Rodolfo had a long talk, with me translating, which I found exhausting. When Beatriz finally offered to drive us back to the hotel, we declined and returned by bus.

During the next two days, we joined in a prayer time at the main Certeza shop, went to the Feria del Libro, an important annual event in the literary life of Argentina, and visited more bookshops associated with Certeza. One evening Len gave a talk on bookselling to a large gathering. Roberto did the translating, giving me a night off.

We were due to fly to Tucuman, a small province in north-western Argentina, on Wednesday afternoon. After lunch with Tony and Priscilla Michael, CMS missionaries working in Lomas de Zamora, we headed for the domestic airport. San Miguel de Tucuman, the capital of Tucuman province, is considered the birthplace of Argentina as an independent federation. We were met at the airport by the manager of Certeza's bookshop in Tucuman, Carlos Yabraian, and his wife, Patricia. They drove us to our hotel, and the next morning Carlos collected us to go to the shop to talk. There we met Carlos's assistant, Juan Manuel Alurralde. Again I was needed as a translator, both at the shop (where there was much discussion) and that night (when Len gave a talk). We had time to visit other bookshops in the city, then met for lunch with all those associated with Certeza in Tucuman, again with much discussion.

By now Len had begun to identify significant issues in the bookselling work he had visited and heard about. He decided to present the problems, as he saw them, along with possible solutions, to the board of Certeza on our return the next day to Buenos Aires.

Getting the report typed and printed was a massive undertaking. Len used a dictating machine; I translated from this and Certeza editor, Adriana, and I put the Spanish version onto computer so that copies could be printed off, collated and handed to board members. We finished late at night and flew back to Buenos Aires the next afternoon. The following day we attended the lunchtime meeting of the board, where Len presented his report. I watched the faces of the board members grow more and more bleak as Len, speaking through an interpreter, confronted them with the need to radically change their operation. Little was said as we left for our hotel.

Beatriz saw us off the next day as we boarded a flight to London. She expressed thanks for the report, saying, "We were peeping over the wall at the future and what to do. You have come in and smashed down the wall. You have given us a fresh start." We left thankful that our United Kingdom trip was to be a holiday.

As soon as we reached London, Len told me to wait with the luggage while he went and arranged the next stage of our journey. He had been dependent on me in Argentina because of the language and I realised he was enjoying being back in charge. The main purpose of our UK trip was for Len to attend a booksellers' convention in Cardiff, Wales, to see some of his friends and to have a holiday. Because Len had recently taken up the honorary role of General Secretary of the Society for Promoting Christian Knowledge Australia (SPCK Australia), we also planned to visit the SPCK headquarters at Holy Trinity in Marylebone Road, London.

Our first stay was with Ainslie and Eppie Thin in Edinburgh. The Thins were bookshop owners like Len, and their daughter had gained work experience at Standard Book in Adelaide. They drove us to Ard-na-Coille Lodge in the heart of Cairngorms National Park. We stopped to climb a "wee mound" on the way—the "wee mound" was about 300 metres high. My waterproof boots didn't fit properly and I only got halfway up before returning to the car. Len and Ainslie completed the climb.

The opulence of our rooms at the lodge was unbelievable. It was in stark contrast to the hotels in Argentina. We luxuriated in the enormous bath with bath bubbles and enjoyed a sumptuous meal with the

Thins. On our way to Stirling, where we were to stay with our friends John and Olive Drane, we visited one of the bookshops the Thins owned in Perth. At Stirling we had a delightful walk around a nearby lake. The whole countryside was so different from the Australian bush.

We had plenty of time to be just tourists for the next ten days or so, going first by train to York, visiting the minster and revelling in the history that dated back to the fourth century, and then to London. Here Len took me to his favourite haunts including Westminster Abbey, St Paul's Cathedral and Madame Tussaud's. We walked beside the Thames to see the statue of William Tyndale, one of Len's heroes. Time was also allocated to meet Pauline Hoggarth, my friend from Peru, who was now working with the mission agency Latin Link. We had an encouraging time with her and Latin Link director John Chapman.

Before heading to the booksellers' convention, we enjoyed time shopping. Len delighted me when he bought me a Raymond Weil watch and spent time helping me buy a dress to wear to the convention dinner.

It was overcast and rainy when we arrived in Cardiff. The number attending was huge—far bigger than our Australian conventions. We had little opportunity to explore Cardiff itself. Princess Anne was guest of honour at the dinner dance, but our table was a long way from where she was seated. When the dancing started, I thought: Now at last Len will dance with me. But no, he wasn't keen, so I danced with one of the other men at our table.

After the convention, we returned to London. I went for a walk and found a special weekend deal at a hotel with a view. We settled there for the few days before we flew back to Australia. Len was returning to his final months at the former Standard Book, now Dymocks.

THIRTY-FIVE

Ministry to the interior

In Peru I had regularly entertained large groups of young people in my home with appetising food. As the oldest of seven children, I had of necessity learned to cook and provide meals in quantity—mostly of the bulk "fill-them-up" type—so I was not daunted by this. In fact, I relished the challenge and delighted in people's appreciation.

During my time of healing in Sydney I did not entertain, but a coupon in a magazine caught my eye, and I thought I could just manage the subscription for the newly announced *Women's Weekly* "Golden Cooking Library". Even in my perplexity, it seemed like something I would be able to use in the future.

In February 1984—still in Melbourne and managing Ridley College bookshop—I had bought a large blank book. As my circle of friends and acquaintances expanded, I felt the need to record my entertaining in order not to be repetitive, and to make room for new experiences. I wrote an inscription in the front:

> Dinner parties, lunches and other occasions where
> I have enjoyed planning the menu, cooking and
> presenting the result.
>
> Delight in the Lord ...
> and he will give you
> the desires of your heart!

The first entry was dated 7 pm, 10 March 1984, at St Kilda. The guests were listed: "Barbara Darling, John & Janine Stewart, Andrew and David, Ros Helmot & Graeme and two sons." Then the menu and wine were listed, followed by my comment on the evening: "Soufflé was excellent as was the chicken roll. Roll took a lot of preparation but was worth it. The desert was a resounding success too. Rounded off with coffee, tea and chocolates. Enjoyable—my first dinner party in Melbourne."

Since that time I have filled seven large volumes covering dinners and lunches held for as few as one and as many as fifteen. Len first appeared as a guest on 26 February 1987. He says that my Melbourne volume lists most of the Anglican clergy who went on to significant ministries in Victoria. While in Melbourne, I did courses in Asian cookery and gourmet cookery: they served me well when I married, as did the "Golden Cooking Library" and the many other cookery books I later acquired.

There is a two-year gap in the hospitality diaries following our marriage. For the first eighteen months of married life, according to Len, I never served the same evening meal twice. He felt it was like living in a restaurant!

Reviewing the hospitality diaries now, I see five distinct strands that emerged over the years.

FAMILY. There were meals and celebrations for Len's family and mine. The first major one was a seventieth birthday party for Len's mother (followed later for her seventy-fifth and eightieth). For each of Len's four grandchildren I created special birthday cakes from the ages of two to twelve, and for several milestones after that. We also hosted parties for my sister Karen's fortieth, and the surprise party I arranged for Len's fiftieth was a standout—as were many Christmases.

BUSINESS. Dinners for Len's business associates or staff colleagues were less frequent, but I found them to be exciting creative opportunities. I offered to cater for a number of staff parties, Christmas lunches and other occasions, when I went mad creating treats for forty to fifty people.

VISITORS. It is astonishing now to see how many visitors to Adelaide, and people visiting or new to our church (Trinity City), we enjoyed sharing meals with. Some became friends, others we never heard from again—but most were enriching occasions.

FRIENDS AND NETWORKS. Entertaining evenings with friends for the sheer enjoyment of each other's company were fun, but we found we could often identify people who might benefit from getting to know others, and enjoyed arranging dinners to watch the results—often gratifying.

MATCH-MAKING. Well, not exactly: but it was interesting how many of our young single friends (and sometimes older ones) enjoyed bringing their prospective partners to a meal and hearing our observations, which seemed important to them.

The creative delight of offering hospitality expanded to new horizons when I was later involved in various organisations. The decade of the 2000s, approximating my time with CMS South Australia and Northern Territory, was one of many overseas house or dinner guests, including those connected with Len's role with SPCK Australia (later renamed SparkLit) and the Australian Christian Book of the Year Awards.

Siblings in Queensland.
1996

THIRTY-SIX

Family responsibilities

I visited my parents in Queensland in March 1992, arriving with a huge bunch of roses from our Adelaide garden. It was a precious time. For the first time I felt I could talk to them adult to adult. I told them I loved them and thanked them for everything they had done for me. I had never been able to do this before.

Mum's illness had progressed and she couldn't speak, but I saw in her eyes that she understood and that any issues we'd had in the past were now resolved. I also saw that she loved me, and somehow knew that she always had, but had never been able to tell me so. I remembered all the things she had done for me and realised that actions were the way she said, "I love you." I thanked her for many specific things.

On 21 June 1992, I phoned my parents at 6 pm. Dad answered, and as we began to talk, Mum rang her bell insistently and began banging. I listened to Dad interacting with her. He came back suggesting that I ring again in five minutes. I did this and was able to tell Mum that I would be visiting her in two days' time before joining Len at the annual Australian Booksellers' Convention. An hour later, Dad phoned again. Mum had died just minutes after I spoke to her.

I flew to Brisbane the next morning. It was a surreal time as the family gathered in our old home with Mum no longer there. We planned the funeral service, which was to begin with my brother Andrew playing "Amazing Grace" on his trumpet. I was privileged to speak and chose the text Philippians 1:21: "For me to live is Christ, and to die is gain." Len was with me at the funeral, but soon afterwards we had to return south for the convention.

I went back to Brisbane as soon as I could in August to help go through Mum's things. Before tackling the job, I spent a few days with Dad, taking him to places I knew were special to him and Mum. We went to Toowoomba to visit Grandma Phyllis' old home, then drove around the town as Dad talked about the past. Each day we shared our Bible reading and prayed together for the family.

Back in Booval, the rest of the family arrived and we sorted through Mum's drawers and wardrobe, each taking something as a remembrance. Everything else we sent to second-hand outlets. Dad gave me Mum's engagement ring. He wanted us to shift some of the furniture around and reorganise his bedroom as there was no longer need for wheelchair access. On our final night we all dined at Alison's. As Dad farewelled me at the airport, I suddenly saw how old and sad he looked. I decided then that we would make his seventieth birthday the next year special.

When I arrived home, I knew I needed some quiet time to come to terms with Mum's death, so I headed for Waterfall Gully and spent some hours wandering in its bushland. As I reflected on my mother, I again realised she showed her love by doing, not saying. I knew I was like her and prayed for the ability to "say" as well as "do" to express my love.

The situation with all three of Len's children had changed over the past year or so. Jenny had given birth to a second child, so Len now had both a granddaughter, Kelly Rose, and a grandson, Maurice Lee. Jenny and Steve had moved back to Adelaide, but they were not happy together and separated. With our help, Jenny bought a small two-bedroom home about an hour's drive from our house. I was able to help her by sometimes collecting the children from school.

Heather had to be rescued from her abusive partner. We immediately suggested she come to live with us. We all went for a short break by the sea, and on this brief holiday I lost my mother's engagement ring at the beach. I was so upset—we searched but it was never found. Back at home, Heather started work at Coles, and Len and I asked her to pay board. We put this money into a special account for her to access when she left. She was with us for nine months. At first I drove her to work, but when her Aunt Margaret left her some money, Len suggested I teach her to drive. This I did, and she was able to drive herself and be more independent. She left our home when she moved in with a new boyfriend, Vince Mastanduono.

Len's son David and Tina were still together, but Tina told me that she often found David very controlling. He was adamant that they should not have children and was deeply involved in growing and selling marijuana. I was thankful that Tina felt confident to share her problems with me. When they visited us, David continued to act as if Grandview Grove was his home, but we realised that as long as he lived in his marijuana-growing house, he would continue to be in and out of prison for drug trafficking.

Len started a new consultancy business and was frequently away from home, travelling as far afield as India, the Philippines and Indonesia. When he was away, I felt more and more responsible for the family. In 1994 he was invited to do a consultation with SPCK India and wanted me to go with him. I wanted to say yes, but I felt that David would benefit from time with his father to further repair their relationship. This turned out to be a very good idea. Observing extreme poverty in India had a profound influence on David and enabled him to survive several spells in gaol.

In 1995, Heather and Vince were delighted to welcome a baby son, James Umberto, into the world. Two years later James's sister, Teresa Brooke, was born. Len loved having grandchildren in his life, and I tried to make it easy for Jenny, Heather and their children to have special times with him. We saw more of Jenny and her two since she lived nearer.

As his consultancy work grew, Len was often away in Sydney or other cities, and I was pleased to be home to support the family. My sister Karen was sadly widowed, and it was good to be living in Adelaide where I could give some support to her and her son, my twelve-year-old nephew James, as well. I kept in touch with my Queensland brothers and sisters too.

1993

THIRTY-SEVEN

Scripture Union South Australia

In 1991, as I was settling happily and enthusiastically into Adelaide life, former SU colleagues asked me to consider becoming chairperson of Scripture Union South Australia. I felt my new status as a wife obliged me to seek Len's approval for this. Being a long-time supporter of SU, he readily agreed.

It wasn't long before he began to question the wisdom of his decision. With my usual tendency to over-invest my time, my new involvement sometimes came into conflict with family responsibilities. I made a mistake in my first appointment of a State Director, who left two years later, and there were many meetings as a result. Ralph Byles took over as Director and did a wonderful job,

There were many challenges. Some on the council were less attuned to our core ministry of providing Bible reading notes and camps focused on teaching Bible stories and their meaning. Work with SU meant much travel, and I attended many meetings in other states as we wrestled with the relationship between the national office and each state's individuality. As a separate issue, Len was called in as a consultant in relation to SU's national distribution centre.

Despite my "over-involvement", Len gave me wholehearted support. In 1993 we entertained the whole council to dinner. My menu of chicken and cheese with lemon sauce, baked potatoes with crème fraîche, carrot and broccoli, and tart flan and cream, along with four different wines (plus soft drinks), was ambitious. But it was very successful, and it achieved its purpose of creating a great environment in which to set some direction for SU South Australia. Home hospitality facilitated tricky meetings.

There were many such occasions, and Len would occasionally protest—not at the food accounts (which he discretely refrained from commenting on) but at the vast amounts of time and preparation I put into them. Later I was appointed to SU's federal management team, which also involved much travel to other states. I loved doing it, and Len was very tolerant.

The work flourished under God. Beach missions and special-purpose camps worked wonderfully, with effective directors, talented staff and enthusiastic volunteers. I worked hard at refreshing the council membership too. The prayerfulness and cohesiveness of the council and committees were deeply gratifying and glorifying to the Lord.

One lesson learned, time and again, was that God never wastes our experiences, good or bad. Despite my sense of failure in Peru, every part of my training and activity there was brought into play as I found myself well-equipped to exercise my roles in Scripture Union. After eight years I felt it was time to relinquish this stimulating involvement, and I concluded my service with SU in 1999.

THIRTY-EIGHT

Trinity Adelaide and Terrace Studies

While Len's family occupied a lot of my time, I also was able to continue my own special ministry at Trinity Church. After the success of the conference I organised in 1992, I led a series of annual Terrace Studies at the church. I loved teaching, and at the same time I was continuing my learning, with Len's support, by completing my Bachelor of Theology studies at the Bible College of South Australia.

Each Terrace Studies series ran one day a week for six weeks. I would teach for the first fifty minutes and then, after morning tea, groups would discuss questions I had prepared. The group leaders and I would lunch together and go through the questions for the following week. This worked well, and I enjoyed the interactions with those who came.

Maundy Thursday? Trinity seemed unaware of it. But I introduced the concept of a Maundy Thursday evening service to Colin Sheehan. He was enthusiastic, and so was our musically talented friend Bill Hague. From 1993 until 2018, this delightful ministry of worship was appreciated.

With both of us being so busy and still trying to learn to communicate better, we occasionally went away for a few days to work through our relationship problems. One time, on Kangaroo Island, our trip began badly. Len was so keen not to be late for the ferry that we left home and arrived at the wharf before the boat preceding the one we were booked on had left the quay. We had a long boring wait, and I let Len know that my timing, not his, was right. It took a couple of days for us to talk through our different perceptions. He was convinced I was to blame for the lack of communication, and I was certain it was his fault.

As the days went on, we relaxed, enjoying the wildlife, beaches and beauty of the island. At night Len would read aloud to me—he liked reading and did it well. On this holiday, he chose chapters from *Out of the Silent Planet* by C. S. Lewis and Stephen Covey's *The Seven Habits of Highly Effective People*.

Both of us made notes from the latter to help us formulate personal mission statements. I wrote a long list of changes I needed to make. My statement began: "Knowing God's forgiveness and restoration to himself through Jesus, I desire with humility, integrity and graciousness to be light and salt to all with the fruit of the Spirit evident in my life." I then listed seven things I would do "to nurture my productive capacity". These included Bible reading and prayer, physical and health habits, mental alertness, and attitudes towards others (ending with "putting aside competitiveness and not seeing others as threats"). I also listed what I would do in my relationships with Len, his children and grandchildren, my family, our friends and acquaintances, and finally in the ministry context.

I could see how helpful it was to think through my habits in detail like this. Working through our relationship difficulties and considering how things could be done better was a truly helpful exercise.

THIRTY-NINE

Peru again—with Len

Early in 1996, SPCK in London asked Len whether he would be available to undertake a consultancy for Libreria El Inca, a long-established Christian bookshop in Lima, Peru. Len was keen, not least because it would give him the opportunity to see the country that had been so significant to me. As it was five years since his 1991 consultancy with Certeza Argentina, a trip would also provide an opportunity for a follow-up visit there, a prospect Certeza welcomed eagerly.

I was excited. Apart from the joy of showing Len "my territory", I knew I would be essential as his translator. So my second return to Peru took place during July and August 1996.

We arrived in Lima several days before Len's official work was to begin. Paul Clark met us and took us to our accommodation in a secure flat provided by El Inca. Len was astonished at the heavy metal grille, solid door and iron cross-bar with three huge locks that comprised the entry to the flats. Theft in the area was a big issue. Basic food supplies had been kindly provided, and we had just settled down to sleep when the building was shaken: Len's first experience of a minor earthquake. He was only mildly reassured next day when he was told that an earthquake on your first day in Lima was a sign of good luck.

During our first day, I received a phone call at the flat from Linda Gamero, one of the participants in our first leadership training course. She was aware it was my birthday in a couple of days' time and invited us to join some friends for an evening meal the following day. When Len asked who would be there, I admitted I had no idea, but I expected possibly five or six people. I was slightly apprehensive—it was fifteen years since I'd left, and ten years since my last visit.

We took a taxi to the address given and were ushered into a room full of people—twenty-six all told, including many of my original band of leadership trainees. There was speculation as to whether Linda's husband Moisés Rodriguez (also one of the original camp leadership trainees) would arrive. He was rarely able to join social gatherings because he was now a colonel in the national police force in charge of anti-terrorism, combatting the brutal Shining Path movement. He did arrive—in good time for the food and celebration!

It was a joyful and encouraging surprise birthday celebration. Len reported that the dinner was like "the return of MacArthur" and said he finally understood how Prince Philip felt. He was thoroughly scrutinised (and approved of), but the language gap kept him from understanding most of the conversations and he was definitely "second fiddle". I was overwhelmed by the number of old friends and trainees, and fascinated to learn what each of them was now doing. Many were still actively involved with Unión Bíblica.

At the conclusion of the party, Moisés Rodriguez took us in his car on a night tour of Lima. Using his police pass, he was able to get us into the forecourt of the splendidly lit Palacio de Gobierno—the residence of the president—with its colourfully uniformed guards.

I enjoyed observing Len's curiosity and delight at the sounds, smells and sights of Lima. I took him to Miraflores to walk past my old residence, Apartment 3, 1370 Jose Parade, and to visit the nearby Parque del Amor (Park of Love). Because of his height, he endured many uncomfortable journeys in *micros* as I took him to central Lima to visit the Museum of the Inquisition, the Cathedral, the Plaza de Armas and other iconic sites in the old city. One special day Paul Clark drove us the long, dry eighty-nine miles south to visit Kawai, the seaside camp where the practical component of our leadership training courses were held. The substantial development since I had last been there—new buildings, grounds and swimming pool—was testimony to a thriving organisation.

Len spent ten intensive days working with El Inca, learning to travel each day to central Lima by either *micro* or *colectivo*. His report, completed and dispatched after we returned to Australia, was significant. During the consultation period, I was asked to deliver two staff training sessions for the bookshop staff. My language proved fluent and the sessions were well received.

On 24 July a reception was held for us at Unión Bíblica. It was a warm and nostalgic time for me. We met the staff and inspected the offices, the meeting hall and the staff kitchen. Unión Bíblica were providing meals and accommodation for street kids, some of whom we met and who enjoyed being photographed with us.

After a visit to the offices of Editorial El Puma, a leading evangelical publishing house, we prepared to leave Lima. But to show Len Peru without visiting Machu Picchu would have been unthinkable. I had visited there with Nancy Black in 1978. Our flight from Lima to Cusco was scenic and straightforward, but the thin air at 3400 metres was challenging. Despite walking gently, before we had even got to lay down at our hotel we were both experiencing the dreaded *soroche* mountain sickness. We were so miserable, but we had been given the phone number of the Davies, two missionary doctors, who were very kind and prescribed cups of coca-tea. Eating was impossible.

Fortunately the symptoms abated somewhat by morning. We rose early to take the incredibly beautiful train journey descending through the Urubamba Valley to Machu Picchu at 2400 metres. The delight of the trip dispelled any remaining thoughts of sickness. We had a very full day enjoying the extraordinary variety of sights and experiences of this amazing fifteenth-century Inca citadel. We returned to Cusco and spent a day exploring the city before returning to Lima.

Next we flew to Argentina. Iguazu Falls, on the border between Argentina and Brazil, had been a fascination of Len's since he saw them in the movie *The Mission*. I had seen them with Nancy Black and was looking forward to revisiting. They more than met Len's expectations. Situated on the Iguazu River, the falls are the largest in the world, and truly awe-inspiring. So are the birds, butterflies and wildlife in the surrounding countryside. We had a joyful couple of days on both the Argentine and Brazilian sides before proceeding to Buenos Aires.

The Certeza consultancy was timely for them. Their circumstances had continued to change, often complicated by changing government policies, bureaucratic burdens and economic crises. Len's report was helpful and welcomed. Our flight home was via Chile's Punta Arenas and the polar route, affording splendid views of the Andes and the Antarctic.

With two mentees at the wedding of a third.
2003

FORTY

Mentoring women

In 1997 Craig Broman (on staff at Trinity) introduced the idea of mentoring to the church. It began in an embryonic way with a few women being approached to be mentors. I was asked to mentor two young women, Amy Just and Emma Riemer. I began by asking them to tell me their life stories, then asking them where God was in it all.

We agreed to meet monthly at our home, with them catching up in between at church to check how each other was going. One day they arrived as I was about to go to the doctor's. I'd totally forgotten they were coming! I invited them in and told them to catch up with each other and said I would be back as soon as I could. That didn't happen again! I became much more diligent in checking my diary.

A short time later, Craig asked if I would take over the mentoring program. I didn't realise the magnitude of the task, but I threw myself into it. I asked a few women to help me come up with ideas. We decided we needed a Bible verse on which to base the program, something that related to and encompassed both the mentors and mentorees. We chose the second part of Colossians 1:28 (CEV) and commenced Trinity Women's Christian Mentoring "So that all of Christ's followers will grow and become mature".

There was much more to do. I approached various women to help develop a statement outlining the objective of our mentoring. Eventually this was defined as:

> Trinity Women's Christian Mentoring is an intentional relationship of trust where Christian women seek to accompany less experienced women as they grow to maturity of relationship with God.
>
> In knowledge—by feeding on God's Word daily.

In experience—by knowing God's grace in daily life and our hope for eternity.

In action—by being women of prayer; serving God's people; communicating effectively with those who do not yet know Jesus.

Next, we worked on identifying the essential characteristics of mentors and mentorees and the tasks of both, then described the essential components of a mentor/mentoree meeting. Finally we added a summary statement:

Trinity Women's Christian Mentoring is one facet of discipling women at Trinity. It is expected that those identified both as mentors and mentorees will be involved in the wider ministry of Trinity and be regularly present at one of the Sunday services. Within the Trinity context, the commitment between mentor and mentoree is for a predetermined period, normally two years.

I put all of this into a document, knowing that having it in writing turned it into both an essential tool for the women involved and something that could be used when recruiting potential mentors. Over the years this document became a sought-after guide for other groups and churches implementing similar programs.

Although I considered two years sufficient to help the mentorees, I didn't allow for the significant friendships that would develop and the desire of mentors and mentorees to keep meeting. I assumed in the beginning that it would be possible to "recycle" mentors to work with other mentorees, but this did not prove practicable.

Finding mentors involved visiting women in their homes and going through the document. The model was to pair one mentor with two mentorees. I travelled far and wide across Adelaide, meeting with both mentors and mentorees. It took much time, but it was wonderfully rewarding as I saw the relationships flourish. In a couple of cases I got the pairings wrong; this necessitated finding a new mentor and splitting the pairing of the mentorees. Eventually all were happy with the mentors they had.

As momentum built, over one hundred women were regularly meeting. I personally mentored several pairs of young women. Women who would not normally have met became firm friends. The opportunity to mentor women from country South Australia often meant that when they met the man of their dreams, Len and I were invited to the weddings. Firm friendships continue to this day.

Coordinating the mentoring gave me opportunities to speak to different groups outside the Trinity network. At Easter 2005 I spoke at a Lutheran camp at Yankalilla, south of Adelaide. I was also given the opportunity to speak to a group of women leaders in Melbourne at a meeting of EFAC (Evangelical Fellowship of the Anglican Church).

Eventually the need to train mentors became obvious. I conceived the idea of getting all mentors and mentorees together for a breakfast twice a year. Rather than having a speaker, I asked eight women of varying ages to share for two minutes on whatever topic we were addressing. Topics ranged from "Patient Perseverance" and "Casting Off and Putting On" to "The Power of Prayer", "Discipleship", "Discipline" and "Accountability". I prayed about each gathering's topic then approached different women each time, giving them the experience of sharing up front. The diversity of contributions was always astounding.

Although I resigned in 2008, the breakfast continued, and from 2015 became an annual brunch. I am no longer involved in mentoring, but I go to the 7 pm service where there are many young people who value having an older person to speak with. It is a worthwhile ministry. I make a point of inquiring about their Bible reading. I ask how many times a week they eat, and when they respond, I say, "You feed yourself physically, how about feeding yourself spiritually?' I find conversations follow on various topics.

I am still occasionally asked to find a mentor for one of the young women. I have mentored several from the 7 pm service. When I resigned, it was with the view that a younger woman would take over, but that did not happen. Yet the relationships and training of those involved over the years since 1997 continue fruitfully today.

Jenny, David and Heather.
2006

FORTY-ONE

Family drama

Mother's Day—10 May 1998—is a date etched in my memory. Len was away in Tasmania and my brother Andrew, his wife, Donna, and their baby, Jessica, were staying with me. I was just waking up at about 7 am when I heard banging on my window.

"Let me in!" a voice demanded. "Let me in!"

"Who is it?" I shouted.

"David! Let me in!"

I put on my dressing gown and went to open the back door of the house. Len's son barged past me, saying, "I must get my bag!"

Before I had time to tell him that people were asleep in the middle bedroom, he had flung open the door and begun to pull at Andrew's backpack so he could stand on it to reach a top cupboard. I stopped him before he ruined the pack, so he jumped and snatched a bag down and then set off for the back door again. I got there first, locked it and held the key.

I prayed, then confronted him. "Where are you going?"

"To wipe out my bloodline."

"Why?"

"To cancel out the curse—the curse on us from our English and Scottish families. It goes back two thousand years!"

On and on he talked. The "bloodline" seemed to include various people at different points in his rambling—sometimes it was the whole family, then Heather was excluded, then his girlfriend's family was included, then Steve's family. Senseless talk, peppered with strong swear words, flowed out of his mouth. None of it made sense.

"You don't understand! You can't understand! It's all true! You don't know what the truth is. You think he"—meaning Len—"is doing one thing, but he's not. You'll see today. Come with me and you'll see what the truth really is. You'll hear it. You'll see it."

I knew David had a gun in the bag, so I had to unlock the door. He told me to get dressed and come with him. I suggested he dismiss the cab he had come in and I would drive him. I tried to ring someone but discovered he had rendered my phone inoperable.

I managed to get a message to Donna to ring Len's "Blokes' Breakfast Group" to tell them what was happening and that David had a gun. David came in to hurry me up. I prayed while dressing. I left without my purse and took off my wedding ring, leaving it on my dressing table.

Lucy, our dog, tried to hop in the car. I put her out, then drove as instructed—as slowly as I could—to his mother's house. He said several times that he was prepared to "do time" if he had to. Thankfully, Judy was not at home. He told me to drive him to his sister Jenny's. I was driving slowly so he shouted, "Drive faster or I'll blow your f—— brains out!" I did, but refused to break the speed limit.

David received a phone call on his mobile as we drove. It was Morgan, with whom he had spent the night drinking. David asked strange questions that Morgan couldn't answer. He became even more agitated. I tried to keep him talking so he couldn't hear the "voices" I suspected were directing him. I suggested that instead of going to Jenny's we could go to the hospital where his mother worked. He seemed to agree at first, but then he said it was to Jenny's we must go.

When Jenny opened the door, he strode in, forcing her back into the kitchen. He began to demand answers from her. She had no idea what he wanted, but she handled him superbly. She told him he had the "key". David responded reasonably at first, but then became more agitated and took out the gun.

Jenny's children, aged five and six, started to scream. I said, "David, the children should not be here." He let me take them out the front door, and I rushed to the neighbours'. I knocked on the door, handed the children over and asked them to ring the police and tell them David had a gun.

When I returned, David was threatening to blow Jenny's kneecaps off if she didn't answer in five seconds, then after another five seconds it would be her guts, and finally her head. Jenny said she couldn't think with a gun pointing at her, so he put it in his back pocket. She stalled him a little longer but he became more agitated. He pulled out the gun again, and as he did so, it discharged. He sat down and said, "I've shot myself." He showed no other emotion. He put the gun on the sideboard and refused to let us treat his wound.

I asked Jenny for a cup of coffee and he let her make one for each of us. Somehow in the talking his mother's name came up, and Jenny suggested she should come down to see them. David agreed, and Jenny phoned her mother at the hospital.

Jenny then said that he ought to explain to his mother what he wanted. As he talked, Jenny fled. The phone call ended and I was left to keep conversation going. Then Judy rang again, spoke to David and suggested he contact a special crisis centre. He passed the phone to me to write down the number for him. As I was doing this, Judy told me STAR Force, the police tactical group, was on the way.

David refused to ring the crisis centre. He just kept saying, "I know what I have to do."

I somehow knew I had to stay with him and keep him talking until help came. I asked him questions and he gave me his version of God and Christianity. I told him that God loved him and so did his dad and the family.

Suddenly he stopped talking and said, "People are coming!" He picked up his gun, disarmed it and walked to the door. There was a lot of blood on the chair he had been sitting on. He got into my car and, as slowly as I could, I got into the driver's seat. Then I heard another voice commanding David to get out of the car and telling me to run.

Police in bulletproof vests with high-powered guns were everywhere. The entire block had been cordoned off. I was directed to a house where Jenny and the children were sheltering. From a distance, I saw that David had been disarmed and was lying face down on the road with a policeman watching him.

Detectives came to question me, and I asked for time to contact Len in Hobart. I rang the people he was staying with, but they explained that at that moment he was preaching. I said it was urgent and that no one had died, but he needed to ring me at Jenny's. He did.

After lengthy questioning by five detectives, I was able to drive home. The detectives recognised that I wouldn't find it easy to drive with the seat beside me stained with David's blood, so they had it cleaned before the hour-long trip home.

Driving with David that morning, I had wondered how Len would react if I died. Now, travelling back home, I thanked God for giving Jenny and me the wisdom that meant no one was killed. Len had let Andrew know he was coming home immediately, but I had to take Andrew and his family to the airport to fly home to Brisbane. After that I visited David's mother Judy, then Len's mother to tell her what had happened. Back at home I had visits of sympathy from Bill Hague and my sister Karen. Then I set off again to the airport to collect Len.

I told him all that had happened, and he wanted to go immediately to see Tina, David's partner, and then to Christies Beach police station to see David. He did not cope well with having to talk to his son through glass using a phone. We finally arrived home at 1.30 am.

David was charged with a number of criminal offences. He was remanded in custody for the next three weeks, when a bail application was made. The bail conditions included him having a psychiatric assessment, but he refused. He was held in custody in the Remand Centre for almost nine months. He kept dismissing his lawyers and hearings kept being postponed. All David's belongings were at our house for the months he was incarcerated, and Len found the mess that his dog and truck made hard to handle. We learnt a great deal about the prison system during this time as we visited David regularly. We prayed he would accept Jesus into his life, and we asked friends to pray for strength for us. David blamed Len and his mother for his problems.

Finally David was charged with illegal gun possession, but there was no penalty. We paid the necessary bail money and he was released to live with us under our supervision for nine months. My relationship with David became quite good during this time. He was respectful and tried to help where he could. When the nine months were over, we bought him a three-bedroom house at Ingle Farm and he moved there to live. It was good to have our home life settled again and back to normal.

It didn't take David long to turn one room of his new house into a marijuana farm. He spent the next few years in and out of prison.

Sometimes he was to blame, but at other times he took the rap for his mates. I wrote regularly to him whenever he was locked up. He often said that the only way he coped with prison life was to recall the abysmal conditions of the poor in India that he had observed firsthand. Even life in prison was better than that.

Lighting the gorilla cake for
Maurice's fifth birthday.
1998

FORTY-TWO
CMS again

Len's anticipation that I would be less distracted when I concluded my service on the SU South Australia Council in 1999 was rather shattered by my acceptance of an appointment to the General Committee of CMS South Australia in 2000. In September two years later, after a council meeting and supper at our home, our South Australia President, Martin Bleby, and General Secretary, Leigh Cameron, lingered at the front door after the other members had left. They told Len they were asking me to succeed Martin as President.

Len turned, looked me in the eye, and said, "You'll have to find somewhere else to live!"

Martin and Leigh looked a bit shocked and departed. Inside we had a "discussion". Len promised to pray about the matter and we went to bed. The next morning he sent the following email:

> Dear Martin & Leigh
>
> Given my uncharacteristic reaction on our front doorstep (I quite surprised myself!!!), I thought it would be good to reassure you that Lesley has my total support in her new role. We had a good talk through the issues later in the evening, and clarified the boundaries in a necessary and helpful way. I really look forward to supporting her participation. She has much to offer.
>
> Len

A whole new vista of hospitality opportunities had emerged!

One of my objectives was to significantly refresh the council with new, enthusiastic and younger faces. It was an exciting time to be reinvolved with CMS, and the objectives were achieved. A major challenge was Leigh's resignation as General Secretary in 2007 and finding his replacement. It was an issue that the refreshed and slightly smaller council worked on and prayed through together.

The State President's role also meant that I served on CMS's Federal Council and, later, Federal Executive, as well as on its candidates, nominations and policy committees. It was wonderful to be part of such a godly and competent team. Of all my roles, working with the new missionary candidates most fully engaged me; it was a privilege to counsel, mentor and encourage wonderfully equipped Christians who were offering themselves to serve God in so many, often difficult, countries.

In 2007, major upgrading of CMS Australia's governance led to the formation of CMS Australia Limited, of which I was a founding director. My formal involvement with CMS South Australia concluded with my appointment as a Federal Vice-President of CMS Australia in 2009. I was nominated as Life-Governor of CMS South Australia, and I found the nomination citation deeply encouraging:

> LESLEY MCGRATH WOODLEY. NOMINATION
> AS LIFE-GOVERNOR OF CMS-SA/NT BRANCH
>
> Lesley McGrath Woodley was President of the CMS-SA/NT Branch from 2002 to 2009. Lesley brought many gifts and skills to the position of President. First of all, her prayerful faith in Christ, and her passion for the gospel. She also brought her invaluable experience as a CMS missionary in Peru for six years, where she pioneered the work of Scripture Union in that country, organising and directing leadership training courses, approximately 40 camps each year, working with teachers and students throughout the year, and publishing support materials. This work has since grown remarkably and brought many people to Christ. Lesley's continuing fluency in Spanish was demonstrated when she interpreted for the guest speaker at SA Summer Encounter in January 2009. Lesley also served as Education Officer with CMS Victoria 1987–89.

Lesley has also served extensively at the Federal level. She became a member of CMS Federal Council in 2002. She served on Federal Executive, and on Federal Candidates, Nominations and Policy Committees. She was appointed as a Director at the inauguration of the CMS-A Ltd Board in 2009, and resigned at the end of January 2010.

Lesley's stated passion is "growing myself and helping others to grow to maturity in Christian faith", together with skill in thinking outside the square and seeking creative solutions.

As Branch President, Lesley was active in seeking out, recruiting, interviewing and mentoring missionary candidates. She led the Branch prayerfully and wisely through the process of finding the person of God's choice in appointing a General Secretary. Lesley was a keen encourager of young people into positions of responsibility in the Branch. She also oversaw the streamlining of the governance of CMS in South Australia.

Two things in particular have stood out in Lesley's service of CMS, that reflect her own priorities and practice. First, whether looking at new missionaries, or new Board or Committee members, Lesley would always ask the question: What is your relationship with Jesus Christ, and how are you sustained in that through the practice of regular Bible reading and prayer? And the other: Lesley would remind us that while money, according to CMS principles, is not in first place, it is in second place, not last! And is to be attended to accordingly, both personally and corporately.

We give thanks to God for Lesley's service of his kingdom through CMS, with the support and approval of her husband Len Woodley.

I have pleasure in nominating Lesley McGrath Woodley for the position of Branch Life Governor.

Martin Bleby
26 September 2010

With Beatriz Buono and friends in Adelaide.
2009

FORTY-THREE

Peru again

In 2005, I received a phone call from Paul Clark asking me to come to Peru and speak at the Second National Conference of Unión Bíblica in South America. Paul's problem—indeed, Unión Bíblica Peru's problem—was that the cohort of volunteers I had trained in the 1970s were all reaching retirement age. He wanted me to speak inspirationally on what it meant to serve as committed volunteers, and on how to train up a new generation of them.

Len encouraged me to go but decided not to accompany me. Business was busy, and he perceived that I would need all my energy for the task. I didn't need the distraction of having to translate for him.

The conference was to be held in early January 2006. We decided that I should fly over on 28 December and stay with Beatriz in Argentina. This would give me a chance to catch up with her and practise my Spanish again before I had to address a large audience. While reading on the flight I came across these words: "Beware of the barrenness of a busy life." I thought of my own life and wondered if I had yet again let myself get so busy that I didn't really connect with people. I prayed that on this trip I would encourage and build people up, and not be judgmental.

I found the journey utterly exhausting and was so thankful to find Beatriz at the airport in Buenos Aires. She took me home and I slept and slept. When she first heard about my visit, Beatriz had asked me to prepare a talk entitled "Thirty Days with God the Father" for a seminar she was arranging. I had spent a long time working on this. Because I had learnt so much myself as I wrote, I coped better than I usually would have when told the seminar had been cancelled. A few years later, someone else needed material on this topic and was pleased to use what I had prepared.

I enjoyed my time with Beatriz, seeing more old historic buildings and shopping in the city. I was interested to see how well she interacted with her employees at Certeza. We had a couple of meals at her daughter's home where we enjoyed playing with her two little grandchildren. I also enjoyed some time with Michael and Elspeth Collie, CMS missionaries working with Certeza, listening to them and encouraging them in the hard but special work they were doing for God. On New Year's Eve I met with other friends and experienced amazing food, fireworks and the unique paper contraptions, lit by candles, that are inflated and released into the sky at midnight. My Spanish improved, and I valued Beatriz's input for the talk I was to give at the conference in Peru.

The four-hour flight to Lima passed quickly. I was met at the airport by Marty Clark. After lunch together, she took me to a seminary to see some friends who were lecturing there. Staying again at her home at Chaclacayo, in the same bedroom that I occupied on my first trip to Peru, brought back many memories. Paul was standing down as the General Secretary of Unión Bíblica after the conference, so I thought this might be my last time in Peru.

The conference commenced on 4 January. I was one of three speakers. My topic was "Contrasting the roles of paid staff and volunteers". John Kessler from Holland (at Kawai in 1956) spoke on "God's role in the history of Kawai" and Mecca Nakachi from Puerto Rico (at Kawai in 1963) spoke on "Working in a team". Two hundred and thirty people attended, representing twenty of Peru's twenty-four provinces.

During the conference, I had the opportunity to talk individually with many young people who sought me out and shared their difficulties. A number of people, whom I had known years before, had positive memories of my ministry and thanked me for what they had learnt at that time. This surprised me; I was still inclined only to remember my failures.

I also enjoyed meeting with Samuel and Lily Escobar again. Samuel was to speak on 6 January and then head for home; Lily was suffering from dementia and was deteriorating fast. Samuel knew she would soon need special care. I prayed for her and asked God to please guard me to the end. I feared losing my memory.

Samuel spent time with me, going through my talk. He suggested certain changes, some of which I made. I noticed that I wasn't affirmed by him, but that didn't worry me in the way it would have in the past. My talk went quite well, and several people thanked me for it. At the Saturday night concert, a small group of young people I had taught to swim blew me away with their thanks.

After the conference, I had a nostalgic trip to Kimo jungle camp with Billy Clark, Paul and Marty's son. We ate traditional soup at La Oroya, experienced the rarefied air of the heights and the huge descent to La Merced, and then crossed on a new cable car to the campsite. It was great to meet old staff there and see the improvements that had been made. We came across a landslide on our return journey to Lima, so the bus had to use the old road, the one I had used in the 1970s.

In Lima I visited the Unión Bíblica offices and had a lovely lunch at my dear friend Berenice's home. I also spent time with Linda Gamero's daughter Lesley, one of three Lesleys in Peru named after me. This trip helped me see that many young people needed mentoring, and I encouraged my older Christian friends to take up the challenge.

Paul Clark was writing a book about Unión Bíblica in Peru. He told me a story of some street kids who stole food and hid in a sewer to avoid the police. The police tried to get them out by using tear gas, but the kids just went deeper into the sewer. One day the police arrived at about dusk with tuna sandwiches and enticed them out with the food. The sandwiches had been laced with poison. One boy, Luis, was not there at the time, and when he arrived, he saw his friends dying. He eventually decided to go to Unión Bíblica and was one of the first of these boys to give his life to Jesus. As Paul told them about the injustice of Jesus' trial and of his death, the street kids wept. They identified with Jesus, who suffered injustice as they did.

Paul also reached out in love to a group of deaf children who were being abused. Unión Bíblica was touching these kids in a profound way.

During the long flight home I had time to reflect on and absorb the things Paul had shared with me. At the conference I had been embraced by 230 Unión Bíblica workers from twenty of Peru's twenty-four provinces who each week worked with thirty-two thousand students. When I arrived in Peru in 1976 I had been alarmed to discover that I *was* "the schools work". I had left Peru in dismay and despair but the leaders I trained, unaware of my fragility and grief, had carried on the work with passion and enthusiasm. God had given the increase; an increase beyond our wildest dreams! Paul Clark named the members of my original group who had been instrumental in bringing God's love to the children of Peru. Sometimes I am very slow to hear and perceive. I had been slow to accept his gentle and persistent encouragement. I prayed for all my Peruvian friends—and thanked God that, in spite of my failure, he had heard my prayers and blessed my five-and-a-half years of ministry among them. By the time I arrived back in Adelaide, the reality had permeated my being, together with an extraordinary peace and deep reassurance of God's love and power. I had a story of transformation and awe to share with Len. Psalm 126:6 says it all.

> Those who go out weeping,
>   carrying seed to sow,
> will return with songs of joy,
>   carrying sheaves with them.

FORTY-FOUR

Family farewells

The eighteen months from July 2007 to February 2009 were emotionally challenging, with funerals for four close family members.

In July 2007 I travelled with Len to a hospital in Ipswich to see my father, who was terminally ill. It was a wonderful visit. Dad shared rich anecdotes, often humorously, and above all encouraged us all with his firm faith in Jesus. We laughed and prayed together. I was very sad, but I felt the time was a special and wholly satisfactory farewell. I spoke to Dad again by phone a few days later while the rest of the family were visiting him. We sang "Jesus Loves Me" together (me over the phone).

Dad, who served with the RAAF from 1942 in Palestine, Cairo and Italy, had come to a lively faith at All Saints Booval under the ministry of Don Douglass. He was an enthusiastic and effective participant in Evangelism Explosion, a Bible study group leader and a great teller of jokes. He passed into the Lord's presence on 29 July 2007. We flew to Brisbane again for the funeral at All Saints. I gave the eulogy and my brother, the Rev Ian McGrath, preached.

Ten months later, in May 2008, Len and I were enjoying a delightful motoring visit to Tasmania when I received a phone call advising that my younger sister Karen, who was in hospital seriously ill with advanced cancer, was probably on the point of death. Accommodation and ferry plans were hastily rearranged to get back to Adelaide in as short a time as possible. I arrived there on 21 May and got to the hospital just before she, too, was received into Glory. Karen had named me as her executor, which subsequently involved many months of work.

Six weeks later, on 18 July 2008, I celebrated my sixtieth birthday. Because I had invited about seventy guests, Len cleverly arranged a "Decade-ent Walk" through rooms of our home, each room decorated with memorabilia and photos from a different decade of my life. It was great fun and a joyful time of gratitude to God.

Earlier that year, after a series of prison terms, Len's son David accepted his mother's offer to stay with her. We felt this was unwise, but in fact it worked well, and she helped him onto an upward path. But it was still very taxing for her. I suggested to Len that we could afford to buy a small one-bedroom unit where David could live independently. In October I located one that was ideal, and David was delighted. He told us that he really wanted a fresh start. We all helped him move in on 2 November.

This happened at a time when a significant change was underway for Len. After sixteen years as the honorary National Secretary of SPCK Australia, he was delighted to be handing over to a paid successor, Michael Collie. Michael and his family had recently returned to Melbourne after sixteen years of service in Argentina with CMS. The transition necessitated moving the SPCKA office from Adelaide to Melbourne, so Michael was due to stay with us later in the month to help pack everything up.

On 4 November—two days after David, supremely happy, had moved into his unit—Len drove me to Adelaide airport to fly to Sydney for a CMS Federal Executive meeting. On the way, he expressed disquiet that he had not received any SMS messages from David for almost twenty-four hours. This was unusual; David was an avid sender of texts to his family. Len decided he would call on him after dropping me off.

As I was actually stepping onto the plane, my phone rang. It was Len. He had just found David dead in his bed. An air hostess helped me off the plane and summoned a taxi for me. On my way to the unit, I phoned CMS to explain my absence. Police, coroner's staff, David's mother and our pastor, Paul Harrington, were all there when I arrived. It was a hard day.

The funeral was delayed by forensics until 13 November. Len assured Michael that he should still come to Adelaide. He did, and also attended the funeral. He was a brilliant help in so many ways, including in the practicalities of hosting the after-funeral refreshments at our home for a large number of people.

With my father, Jim McGrath.
1998

David with Arab.
2005

Three months later, in February 2009, we had the delight of Beatriz Buono staying with us during a visit from Argentina. She was to speak at several CMS conferences around Australia. A few days after her arrival, Len's mum, who lived in a unit quite near us, became desperately ill, so we brought her to be with us. Her heart was struggling and her lungs were filling with fluid. Beatriz assisted me with the messiness of nursing. Two days later, with Len assuring her she had fought the good fight and finished the race, and that we were there to see her safely depart to receive the crown of righteousness, Margaret Woodley literally died in Len's and my arms, as Beatriz prayed. Beatriz also wrote a beautiful reflection on Margaret's life.

The remarkable circumstance by which we were supported in David and Margaret's departures by strong Argentine connections did not escape us. The presence of Michael and Beatriz was a source of comfort and encouragement, not just to us but to our whole extended family. God is so kind.

In the years that followed, our guest bedroom was used for further longer-term family accommodation. My nephew James Mitchell stayed with us for several months in 2010 and 2011 after completing pilot training with MAF (Missionary Aviation Fellowship) via the Melbourne School of Theology. He was working shifts as ground crew for Tiger and Virgin Airlines as he awaited a pilot opportunity. He entertained us, and sometimes appalled us, with behind-the-scenes airline tales.

Len's grandson James Mastanduono lived with us from 2012 to 2014 while completing Years 11 and 12 at University Senior College, overlapping with his sister Teresa, who lived with us for all of 2013 to 2015 while completing her studies at Temple Christian College. I worked very hard at tutoring both of them, and often joked that I'd done my matriculation exams three times!

Unión Bíblica conference, Lima, Peru. 2015

FORTY-FIVE

CWCI

Back in 2006 I had received an invitation to join the panel of speakers for the women's ministry Christian Women Communicating International (CWCI)—often best known through its Know Your Bible (KYB) Bible study groups. I relished the opportunity and promptly accepted.

Over the next ten years I received many speaking invitations from across country South Australia and even Broken Hill. Because each local CWCI committee or organising body advises the prospective speaker of the topic, each engagement required preparation from scratch. Not being a person who can "recycle" without major amendments, that suited me fine.

In CWCI, speaking tours are known as "safaris". My safaris included Murray Bridge (2007); Broken Hill (2010); Kangaroo Island (2011, accompanied by my lifelong friend, Barb Darling); the Limestone Coast, Keith, Bordertown, Kingston SE, Mount Gambier (2015); Broken Hill Women's Convention (2015); and Murraylands (2016). Topics ranged from "Born free: Freedom through forgiveness" and "Real life is about transformation" to "How to drought-proof your life". Each of these journeys involved multiple engagements in a variety of churches and homes.

Life in Australia's country towns can be delightful, but also tough. Christians can feel outnumbered and isolated. Opportunities to participate in Christian activities, visit other churches or experience fellowship more widely than in the local community are limited by isolation. One of the most pressing issues is that, in smaller congregations and communities, there are few people and many tasks, so burnout is common.

This means that CWCI conventions and country teaching safaris are enthusiastically welcomed. My talks were received warmly and almost always resulted in one-on-one conversations over meals or coffee, and sometimes, by invitation, in homes afterwards. Very deep issues frequently emerged. Problems of quiet desperation can sometimes be more easily shared with a trusted visitor than in one's own small community. At times I felt that the after-event conversations might have been more significant than the well-prepared talks!

Inevitably I found myself on various CWCI committees. I enjoyed the rich fellowship among the teams and was inspired by the creativity and energy of many Christian country women.

In 2015, through lack of anyone else being available, I was appointed safari administrator for South Australia's southern region. My responsibility was to organise the safaris in detail and maintain the voluminous associated paperwork. The paperwork drove me mad, and I did it poorly. An organiser of events I may be, but an administrator? No! I'm sure I disappointed the committee, but it was not my talent, and I resigned the role in 2018.

I happily remained on the speakers' panel, though. My last safari was to South Australia's Eyre Peninsula in March 2019, speaking in Cowell, Cleve, Tumby Bay, Port Lincoln, Ungarra and Whyalla.

FORTY-SIX

Farewell to Peru

When I returned home from Peru in 2006, I realised how privileged I had been to revisit the country three times since my original missionary service there. I was not expecting to go again. An email from Paul Clark in mid-2014 was a surprise. It was another invitation to speak, this time as one of several international speakers at the Third National Conference of Unión Bíblica Peru in March 2015.

This was a bit tricky because we had Len's granddaughter Teresa living with us while she did her final secondary school years, and I was supporting her in her studies. Len and I thought an absence of two weeks was workable. The schedule would be intense, but I said yes. The conference was scheduled for 8–14 March.

After nine years away, I was hesitant about my Spanish coming through immigration, but my fluency quickly returned. Reacquainting myself with Peruvian traffic was jarring—driving was even more challenging than I remembered, with cars travelling at 130 kph and trailing one another with no space between. Lanes, where they existed, were simply ignored. I was thankful that friends were praying for me to be calm and safe. I was amazed that I was.

One hundred and sixty-eight people came for the conference, which was designed to strengthen the relationships between the country's different Unión Bíblica groups, ministries and regions. The theme was *Somos Familia* (We Are Family). I felt it was extremely successful in achieving its purpose. My hour-long address on how to ensure volunteers remained long-term went better than I could have hoped for. I did not stumble over words, and my PowerPoint presentation of forty-one slides was well synchronised by a skilled operator. Everyone was attentive and receptive. Paul told me later it was the best talk on volunteers he had ever heard.

The level of engagement in the workshops following my talk was astounding. It was a real test of my Spanish as I needed both to communicate and to understand people's questions and responses. I believe God spoke. Throughout the conference, person after person sought out one-on-one discussion, with openness, responsiveness and a desire to see God transform their lives. There were deep individual conversations, often with tears.

Four things about this trip stood out to me as significant answers to prayer. The first occurred on the Friday before the conference, when I caught up socially with some who had worked with me in Peru thirty-nine years before. I challenged one of the men to come to the conference, and he did. He had been through a tough time and was looking for new direction. He reconnected as a volunteer, and I felt confident he would remain connected.

The second was that at the closing ceremony on the last night, I was not singled out for recognition, but thanked as one of the family who had contributed. God got the glory and not the speakers.

The third resolved after the conference. I had realised that one of the ladies who spoke to me needed a mentor—someone strong enough to challenge her. I was perplexed as to how to arrange this, but on my last day in Lima I caught up with three old friends. Two had been on the Camps Committee when I was first in Peru and were older than me, but the third had been quite young when she participated in the camp leaders' course we ran in 1980. She was now a teacher in her fifties and the perfect match for Katherine, so I put them in contact.

Lastly, back in Adelaide I found that Len and Teresa had coped very well indeed. I considered the conference my "farewell to Peru" journey. I was so deeply encouraged to see the way God had multiplied, over and over, the investment I had made in people as I sought to know Jesus and to make him known.

By the time Len collected me from the plane at Adelaide airport on 19 March, I had succumbed to a nasty infection, which resulted in significant illness and weight loss over the next six weeks. But I was thrilled to have had the opportunity to see the fruit that was such a testament to the prayers of God's people over many years.

Kawai.
2015

The Mediterranean.
2016

FORTY-SEVEN

2016 Jubilee year

Our constant involvements with one organisation or another meant that we never seemed to have the opportunity for extended vacations. Early in 2015, Len felt that we needed to proclaim 2016 a "Jubilee Year", one in which we relinquished all responsibilities for twelve months. This would make a decent holiday possible. I didn't really like the implications, but I agreed—until the next speaking invitation arrived! In fact, over the following months I received a number of requests for involvement during 2016, but Len was adamant. Jubilee!

Putting the plan into action wasn't straightforward. Because neither of us had ever been interested in travel for travel's sake, we didn't have a stimulus for planning. So we simply enjoyed some leisurely road trips—in March to Canberra, Thredbo and Cooma in the Snowy Mountains, then later to Wagga and Melbourne. We checked out galleries and museums and caught up with friends, including Jason Page, who had married us twenty-seven years before and was now ministering with his wife, Ann, at St Peter's Weston in Canberra. We visited an old friend of mine, Neville Bryan, and his wife Kim, as well as Len's cousin Ted Woodley and Ruth.

In August we made another leisurely road trip to Melbourne to attend the stimulating annual presentation of the Australian Christian Book of the Year awards, organised by Michael Collie.

But nothing more extended was planned until Len spotted an email invitation to a special celebration in London. It came from All Souls Church, Langham Place. The event was the fiftieth anniversary of the release of the contemporary songbook *Youth Praise* in 1966. It seemed a slender event on which to build a trip overseas, but it was just the excuse we needed. The focus would be people.

Our September and October 2016 trip was a delight from beginning to end. We started near the Arctic Circle and moved slowly southwards.

In Scotland's Orkney Islands (my first visit to the part of the world from which Len's paternal grandmother had emigrated in 1912), we enjoyed rich fellowship with his many cousins on the island of Westray as their guests at the family's old stone farmhouse Chalmersquoy. The magnificent wild scenery, long visits to twelfth-century St Magnus Cathedral in Kirkwall, visiting active archaeological digs of Neolithic villages and making lovely final visits to three cousins who have since died all combined to make this visit special.

Next we went south to Glasgow to stay with John and Olive Drane. They royally entertained us and showed us the delights of Glasgow, the Antonine Wall, the Falkirk Wheel, the Kelpies and more. We walked along the magnificent West Highland Way from John and Olive's home to Milngavie Station, and enjoyed the equally magnificent scenery of the West Highland Line railway from Glasgow to Oban and back.

A visit to Stirling Castle was followed by lunch with some old Peruvian colleagues, Clive and Ruth Bailey. After so many years without contact, we shared a rich renewal of fellowship.

We then headed to Tayport in the Kingdom of Fife, to stay with my dear friend from Peru days, Pauline Hoggarth. Pauline's hospitality included nature walks, visits to Kelly's Castle and its remarkable vegetable gardens, and a visit to the fish and chip shop in the lovely harbour at Anstruther. A treat for Len was when Pauline took us to see Malcolm Jeeves (then in his nineties, but still professionally active), who many years before had been the Foundation Professor of Psychology at Adelaide University. Len was able to quote to Malcolm the text he had preached from at Unley Park Baptist Church forty-five years previously.

In Edinburgh we had a lovely reunion and dinner with our old bookselling friends, Ainslie and Eppie Thin, toured the Royal Yacht *Britannia* and visited the curious underground town surviving from sixteenth- and seventeenth-century Edinburgh.

Driving from Glasgow to Keswick in the Lakes District, we stayed at the Bridge Hotel in Buttermere. Several days exploring meant that we became quite skilled at negotiating extremely narrow, hedge-lined roads and enjoying long lakeside walks.

Why did we then drive to Sutton Gault? Because it was the nearest accommodation we could find to Ely Cathedral, which Len had wanted to visit ever since reading *Tom's Midnight Garden* to his children four decades earlier. It was also the perfect place from which to enjoy the historic fascinations of Cambridge.

From there we drove to central London, where we stayed in Aldgate. Ten o'clock on Saturday morning, 15 October, found us at All Souls Langham Place, ready to participate in "Jubilate Celebration—Fifty Years Since *Youth Praise*". Sessions with Michael Baughen, Timothy Dudley-Smith, Noel Tredinnick, Daniel Pocock and Chris Idle were part of a well-constructed program. The music was brilliant. It was a superb day when I was challenged and encouraged—a real highlight for us both.

The following day we spent in Greenwich at the Observatory, the Royal Maritime Museum, Inigo Jones's Queen's House and *Cutty Sark*. The next day we enjoyed London's parks and visiting the War Cabinet Rooms in Whitehall.

Finally we headed to Spain. Our plane touched down in Valencia on 18 October, and we stayed in the city centre, marvelling at its marble paving and streets lined with orange trees. I was looking forward to seeing Samuel Escobar, my encourager and mentor in Peru. He came in the evening to walk us to the home of his daughter, Lilly Esther, for dinner. Lilly had prepared a feast!

We found that Samuel was an enthusiast not just for ministry and evangelism, but also for historic Valencia. He called for us at 10.30 next morning and took us for an all-day walking tour of the city's Old Town. We saw pre-Christian Roman streets and abundant fifteenth-century architecture. In his eighties, he exhausted us! He was a deeply knowledgeable guide, and Len perceived his delight in my company.

The next day was an opportunity to visit and encourage the Lovells, CMS missionaries based in Valencia. With them we enjoyed a huge traditional paella. Another afternoon with Lilly Esther and her family finally brought me to a beach on the Mediterranean Sea, so I took off my shoes and paddled, just so I could say I'd been in it.

Madrid was our next stop. We travelled by fast train (300 kph) and stayed in the lovely, modern Jardines de Sabatini apartments, which look directly at the Palacio Real (Royal Palace). From there we explored Madrid. The queues for the Museo del Prado were daunting, but we persevered and had a wonderful day there, as we did at the Palacio Real. I loved using my Spanish, though a few unfamiliar words defeated me.

Twelve months before this journey, I had been contacted via Facebook by Isabel Brando. Isabel was one of the original group of young people, "The Miraflores Group", I mentored in 1980. I had not heard anything of her since, so being contacted by her was a surprise. It was also a thrill, because she attached her ministry newsletter to let me know that she was a missionary for the Iglesia Alianza (Alliance Church), serving in Madrid. She said that what inspired her to become a missionary was knowing me thirty-five years earlier. I found that an extraordinary and humbling encouragement.

She was keen to catch up when we were in Spain, and a train journey to Fuenlabrada brought us to her tiny apartment, a very warm welcome and a lovely meal. She was facing a discouraging time in the church to which she was attached, and I felt privileged that she was able to open her heart to me. There were no obvious solutions, so I could only share my own experience of trusting God in trying circumstances, confidently depending on him for answers.

We returned to London for our flights back to Australia. As we sat at Heathrow, Len asked me what in the whole trip had benefitted me most. I said, "Three things: Michael Baughan's prayers at the Jubilate Celebration; seeing Lilly Esther and talking with her; and catching up with Isabel."

I asked Len the same question. He reflected on Samuel Escobar, Michael Baughen, Timothy Dudley-Smith and others. Then he added, "Seeing older people's energetic involvement in Christian work." He was encouraged by the active faithfulness and energy of those people.

It had been a refreshing and enriching journey.

FORTY-EIGHT

Encouragement from Peru

On 12 January 2017, Paul Clark sent me the following extract from his history of Unión Bíblica Peru. Here is my translation of the chapter "For such a time as this".

> Lesley McGrath: Woman of contrasts. Highly educated and at the same time at home with the unsophisticated. Demanding of herself, yet tolerant of the weak. Able student of the Scriptures, yet able to explain them at rudimentary levels. Outgoing, and yet also introspective. Quiet and gentle, serious when she needed to be, and good fun when not. As Ecclesiastes says, "there is a time for everything".
>
> Her first days in Peru were spent with us in Chaclacayo in the winter of 1976. But we all knew that she should live in Lima. She needed her privacy, freedom to come and go as she pleased and a place to make her own. And with her innate generosity, she needed space to share with others.
>
> Eventually she found an apartment in the perfect place—the penultimate block on Pardo Avenue in Miraflores, with a distant sea view.
>
> We went out to the terrace. "Look," I said, "there in front of you is the Pacific Ocean. Yours twice. At one end your homeland, on the other your adopted one. If you get homesick for Australia, start swimming. Thirteen thousand kilometres and you're home!"
>
> For the good of Unión Bíblica and the work of God on this side of the big pond, Lesley opted for the bustle of life in Peru—not for swimming! She remained for five

good years. Her achievement in that short time is recorded, not on the shifting sands of Kawai or the sometimes-polluted waters of Mantaro River near Chupaca, but in the lives of many, who in turn participated in the multiplier effect that adds up in eternity.

I ponder, with conviction, using Mordecai's words in Esther chapter 4: "And who knows if for an occasion such as this you came to Peru?" Time gives us the answer. I wanted to do everything yesterday, but it was Lesley who reminded me that America was not discovered in one day.

It was the first and only year of Petronio Allauca as director of the movement; he was a good man, but God had other plans for his life. His departure gave Lesley carte blanche to develop her ministry. She started on the right foot. She walked at a steady pace but was never hurried. Her personal appeal and her way of being attracted people to her like bees to honey.

She took up the role and ran. It gave the impetus and opened the door for her to organise the first camp in the new Kimo. "New Kimo" sounds like something bigger and better. It was good, it was really wonderful—but "improved" it was not! In Australia she would not have known anything so primitive!

For the majority of parents of campers, Kimo was still the "Green Inferno". A visitor described it as "the only place in the world where so many insects live for the sole purpose of using you to settle on and eat you alive; where the rivers are full of contaminated fish and carnivorous piranhas; where nights are dominated by an army of mosquitoes, spiders hunting in the dark, and crawling things devouring everything in their path".

Lesley, accompanied by Nancy Black as a guide, set out to prove them wrong, and led the way. She was the

Crossing the Chanchamayo River.
1977

I meet the first of three Lesleys.
1986

first to ride the *huaro* (hand-powered cable car) that crossed the torrential Chanchamayo River, and the first to climb up the steep hill that borders the Inoki Creek to the area of the old avocado plantation with its rustic and dilapidated cabin. (One year later, very young Idelfonso, son of Linda and Moisés Rodriguez, would fall from the second floor through a hole in the insect-ridden planks.) Cooking was done on a wood stove beneath a building consisting of four poles and a palm-thatch roof. Toilets? It was a matter of finding somewhere suitable.

This first camp marked the start of Kimo being the preferred destination for thousands of intrepid campers for decades to come. It was not by chance. I learned that just as God had a plan for Lesley, so he had one for Kimo.

The Kimo experience helped Lesley realise that her contribution would be in the area of training—something no one had given any attention to before. She began with a memorable leadership seminar focusing on training for camp leadership. It was held in Chaclacayo in May 1977, with an attendance of forty-three people. That event gave impetus to our request to the Board that Lesley's idea for an entire training course should become a reality. It did—with great success.

Every Tuesday for two-and-a-half months, potential leaders gathered for teaching and practical experience. The expectation was that, after the course, all would then be trainee leaders in a camp the following summer in order to receive a certificate of completion of the course. The course was repeated in 1980 and 1981 with the same successful results. A practical in Kimo was added to the practicals in Kawai.

To better "feel the pulse" of Peruvian students and to penetrate cultural differences, Lesley chose to work in a school for a time in her area of Physical Education.

It was an enriching learning experience. But the most challenging experience was what happened to her in Kawai in the summer of 1980.

It was the last day of the camp, which was to include a "treasure hunt", a fashion parade with costumes made from newspaper, and a beach bonfire. Suddenly someone came running: "Señorita Lesley, Yolanda has died!" Yolanda was the daughter of our dear neighbours, the Avalos Asin, and a member of the camps team, working in the kitchen. She so admired Lesley that she gave her name to one of her daughters (as also in the future would both Ada Roman and Linda Gamero).

Yolanda had died on the operating table, a victim— I am told—of a physician who took advantage of her poverty to coax her with gifts and then used her as a guinea pig for his profit. Lesley was told that the body was en route from Lima. Meanwhile she had to attend to the camp. At the bonfire, a young leader unexpectedly said: "We have heard testimonies this week from all the leaders with the exception of Lesley. Lesley, please, we want to hear your testimony."

"Lord God, give me words. I have nothing left," she begged. How great was her surprise and gratitude to God when, minutes afterwards, seventeen campers expressed their desire to follow in the footsteps of Jesus.

Without question, the funeral, with its confusion and disarray, and the ensuing wake immersed Lesley in the darkest side of Peruvian life for those who have so little.

If Lesley had only mentored two people, her investment would have been worthwhile. I refer to schools workers Leonor Acosta and Linda Gamero. In both, Lesley invested hours, days, heart and soul. They say "press a single button, then watch the results". Those results can be seen now—thirty years later—in the schools of Chile and Peru.

I learned that in a coal mine, sometimes only one diamond is found. Here are two, and I continue counting them.

So it was that Lesley learned much but taught more. She left her mark. She came to Peru and left when her work was completed.

As in the lives of your students, Lesley, your five years in Peru will be remembered by many and multiplied in the Kingdom.

"Rest from her labour, for her deeds will follow her." (Revelation 14:13)

I learned!

Paul Clark
Lima 2017

Hurtle Square.
2021

FORTY-NINE

A big move, a big birthday ... and a big surprise

Number 37 Grandview Grove, Toorak Gardens, was a delightful 1920s Adelaide bungalow with eight rooms. Len had purchased it in 1969, and I had lived there since 1989. From time to time we discussed "downsizing". We recognised that if either of us had a significant medical setback, the large house would become a burden. I fell in love with every smaller place we looked at, but Len always found something not quite right. In the end I said, "Don't show me anything else until you've made up your mind!" He decided to stay put.

One Saturday in March 2017, as he was browsing the local community newspaper, he saw a photograph of some lovely modern bookshelves. On closer reading, he noted that they were in an apartment for sale on Hurtle Square, right in Adelaide's CBD—somewhere he had no desire whatsoever to live. But those bookshelves intrigued him, so, respecting my wishes, he discretely attended the open inspection that afternoon. He was impressed enough to suggest that I look at it with him the next day, and I did. It was perfect—not least because Len calculated that the shelves could accommodate approximately half of the 6000 books we had at home.

We made a successful offer, but for various reasons—including the need for renovations and a crisis of confidence about the purchase on Len's part—we didn't actually move in until April 2018. I loved it immediately, and after he'd settled down, Len did too.

My seventieth birthday a few months later was a big test. We had invited up to seventy guests to significant parties at our old home, and my birthday list was easily over fifty ... until Len pointed out that fifty was impossible. I had such a hard job of pruning that list! But

12C Hurtle Square proved most adequate to comfortably entertain thirty guests, and I enjoyed a lovely celebration of God's kindness and faithfulness to me over seven decades.

Another aspect of God's kindness, which we were not at that point aware of, was in providing a much more manageable home.

In the months following my birthday, various friends started asking Len, "What's wrong with Lesley?" He was only mildly aware—and I was totally unaware—that my demeanour appeared to others to be angry, or sad, or depressed. I was none of those things, but during the following year a number of other symptoms emerged. They needed investigation.

My GP referred me to a geriatrician, and in December 2019 I was diagnosed with dementia. The symptoms were consistent with frontotemporal dementia (FTD). When the geriatrician asked me whether I was anxious, I said: "No. 'Do not be anxious about anything, but in every situation, by prayer and petition with thanksgiving, present your requests to God. And the peace of God which transcends all understanding will guard our heart and mind in Christ Jesus.'" He was rather surprised!

Although it may be several years away, I have planned my funeral service. It is to conclude with the hymn I chose for my first commissioning for service in Peru, and which sums up my desire for others:

> Go forth and tell! O church of God, awake!
> God's saving news to all the nations take.
> Proclaim Christ Jesus, Saviour, Lord and King,
> That all the world his worthy praise may sing.
>
> Go forth and tell! God's love embraces all;
> He will in grace respond to all who call.
> How shall they call if they have never heard
> The gracious invitation of his word?
>
> Go forth and tell where still the darkness lies,
> In wealth or want, the sinner surely dies:
> Give us, O Lord, concern of heart and mind,
> A love like yours which cares for all mankind.

Go forth and tell! The doors are open wide:
Share God's good gifts, let no one be denied.
Live out your life as Christ your Lord shall choose,
Your ransomed powers for his sole glory use.

Go forth and tell! O church of God, arise!
Go in the strength which Christ your Lord supplies.
Go till all nations his great name adore
And serve him, Lord and King, forevermore.

James Seddon
1915–1983

Acknowledgements

In 2015 I realised that I had over forty volumes of handwritten diaries, starting from when I was eight years old. As I got older, the diaries also became prayer journals in which my questions, prayers, answers, thoughts and struggles were recorded in detail.

I read my first missionary story at the age of eight. Many have been inspired over the years by missionary biographies like *The Small Woman* (about Gladys Aylward), *Green Leaf in Drought* (about Isobel Kuhn) and *Through Gates of Splendour* (about Jim Elliott). My own story was not in any way comparable to those, but as I continued to mentor younger women, I felt that some of them might find useful lessons from my life. So I began to reduce those forty handwritten volumes into a long story. The resulting 190,000 words was not a publishable book, but it was a comprehensive memoir, appreciated by family members and a few close friends.

By 2019 I realised that I could not progress it further. An offer by Margaret Douglass to turn the memoir into a book was generous, timely and extremely welcome. I mailed her the three wire-bound volumes which had been printed at home. This book is the result of her work.

Margaret had much to do with me and my family when I was in my teens. Her husband, Don, was the rector of our church, All Saints Booval, and she was intimately engaged with the parish families. For her to have turned my memoir into something publishable was a huge effort for which I cannot adequately express my gratitude.

I am also deeply indebted to so many friends who, at various points of my life's journey, have encouraged, supported and challenged me or deeply shared my trust in Jesus. A few have been mentioned by name, but so many have not. All of them have shared in the experience of having faith, being flawed, and yet finding that God has blessed their work with the fruitfulness of bringing people to faith, or of strengthening people's faith in the Lord Jesus Christ, to whom be all glory.

Lesley McGrath Woodley
Adelaide 2021